FOREWORD BY:
DR. DARRELL WILSON

LIFTED

ALLISON N.
WILEY
WITH SHIRLEY CARNEY

Lifted

Published by:

Embassy Publishing

P. O. Box 6003

Fort Worth, TX 76115

email: embassypublish@aol.com

Phone: (817) 213-7767

ISBN 978-0-9837373-1-5

DEDICATION

This book is dedicated to the masses that have traveled a road that spiraled downward while their soul cried out to be lifted. This testimony is for those who need God to loose them from their enemies, to lift them high above those who rise against them, and to be delivered from violent situations. Be *Lifted!*

ACKNOWLEDGEMENTS

TO:

God Almighty… my Glory and the Lifter of my head…
without You I would have perished.

My children… my breath, my being, my heart… may you
understand the true meaning of faith. May you NEVER repeat
the mistakes of your father or your mother.

John… the best father I know, my friend… we went through a
storm together. The Lord is with you.

Daddy, Ma Wiley, and Zita… my survival kit… with you on
my side, I was never alone… thank you can never say it all.

TO:

Jackie's family and friends… she was my angel… she is
always with me. I can't stop loving her.

Wendell Wilson and family, Dana Sanusi… you never left my
side. You are true friends indeed.

Pastors Bridget and John and Zion Covenant Ministries… your
prayers pushed me through.

Dr. Phillip Phinn… your prophetic gift pulled me out.

Dr. Darrell Wilson… for insisting that I tell the story.

Shirley Carney, Etoyce Davis, Elinor Jackson… for helping me
find my voice… for giving me the words. Many thanks.

Foreword by Dr. Darrell Wilson

Lifted, an excellent body of work by Dr. Allison Wiley, the mother of four beautiful children, Pharmacist, Entrepreneur, Business Executive, Humanitarian, and a Non-Governmental Organization Ambassador to the United Nations, chronicles her journey of life as a woman with a unique sense and grasp of destiny and purpose.

As my wife and I read this book, we found ourselves hanging on to every word, almost unable to put it aside until we had finished the very last page. Allison's candid approach allows the reader to share her quest to overcome unprecedented life challenges, while she struggled to trust, believe, and develop a strong persevering faith in God. I must warn you that once you start reading, you will not want to put this book down until you have finished it.

Lifted gives reality to the English Poet Alexander Pope's famous quote, **To err is human, to forgive is divine.**

In the fall of 2010, my wife and I participated in a leadership conference in Nassau, Bahamas. One of the sessions we attended was led by a distinguished panel of businessmen and women. At the conclusion of the session, time was allotted for a question and answer session. Dr. Wiley approached the microphone, introduced herself, and stated her home-town as being Houston, Texas prior to posing her question to the panel. Being a native Texan, I felt a sense of camaraderie and followed her question with sincere interest. It was apparent that she had given significant thought to presenting her question with passion and grace, fully expecting the panel to take note and respond in kind.

At a later time during that same conference, my wife and I were personally introduced to Dr. Wiley by a mutual friend. Several weeks afterwards, we again met her while visiting Dallas. Since that time, we've gotten to know her better and in so doing, believe her story is one that must be shared with the world.

Lifted is written at such a pace that you will experience the reality of a sense of injustice, devastation, abandonment, disappointment, humiliation, discouragement, and betrayal. Concurrently the results of encouragement, nurture, perseverance, strength, hope, and restoration flow with equal speed. Above all, you will experience a joy of the spirit that transcends all else.

Be *Lifted!*

Dr. Darrell Wilson is the Senior Pastor and Founder of Acts Church Ministries International based in Fort Worth Texas where he ministers with his wife, Lady Njideka Wilson. He is also the President and CEO of Embassy Publishing, and is a member of the Executive Council of the International Third World Leadership Association under the Direction of Dr.Myles Munroe

CHAPTER 1

Already the house had begun to smell of deceit, disappointment and decay. I lowered myself to the floor after coming through the back window, stealing my way inside like a thief in the night. It was my house. It would take more than a lost appeal for that not to be so.

I had been crying for days and had no intention of shedding any more tears tonight. This was my house and I was going to come home to it every day. I didn't care about the big padlock on the front and back doors. Locks were for honest people and the courts had told the entire world that my husband was a criminal. Like a child I thought to myself, whatever they said about him rubbed right off of him and on to me. The courts painted my entire family with the same brush they'd used on John.

Well, there were more ways to skin a cat than one. The courts could take my husband, and my house, but I would survive anything they threw at me.

Without turning on the lights, I moved freely from one room to the next inhaling old familiar scents, dazed with memories. What had happened to the life we'd shared in this house? The noise in my head was what grief sounds like, and I closed my eyes to let my life in this house wash over me.

I eased into the room where we were the happiest. At my mother's house that room had been the kitchen, but for us it was appropriately called the family room. Squirreled on the floor with the ceiling fan running overhead, I closed my eyes and rocked with the memories that came rushing from every corner of the house. Tiny arms around my neck. Baby kisses. My beautiful little girl twirling on tippy toes. I could feel John's arms circle my body from behind to hold me and the baby close, his lips playfully kissing both of us.

Christmas time was better in this room than any other place on the face of the earth. The Christmas tree stood in the far corner to the left and was decorated with special ornaments. One for each child for each year, every Christmas. Presents knee deep for all of our family and friends who came to celebrate Christmas Eve at our house. I loved Christmas. I loved this house. It had been my first home since leaving Trinidad and Canada. Every place else had merely been a place to stay. Moving had not been in my plan and being evicted from a house that we had already paid for was unthinkable.

CHAPTER 2

John and I knew we were made for each other. We were soul mates. There was a point in time that I thought I could never love anybody with the intensity that I loved him. We had been finishing each other's sentences for years. Our personalities naturally complemented each other, we laughed at the same things, thought football was created just for us, liked Mexican food, but could not tolerate hot peppers. How lucky we were to meet each other in pharmacy school.

John had a certain amount of stick-to-it-ness that I had a healthy respect for. He knew what he wanted to do with his life and had a plan for getting there. The plan was always uppermost in his mind and if I'd wanted to hear it every day, he'd run it down for me. First, he was going to finish school with the best grades possible, then, he was going to strike out on his own and make his fortune. He wanted to own a chain of pharmacies and was determined to make his dream come true even if he had to start small.

My goals were a lot more immediate but still as lofty. I wanted to get good grades so that I could get a scholarship to continue my education without paying hefty foreign student fees.

He was tall and lean and walked with a certain smoothness. Handsome didn't quite describe his appeal. He had charm and style; commodities I found to my liking. I had never met a guy quite like him. Even so, he didn't sweep me off my feet. Instead, he wooed me with his dreams.

We spent as much time together as our schedules permitted. That often meant short picnics beneath a huge oak tree near the College of Pharmacy and Life Sciences. Neither of us had the money to venture far from campus. It was beneath this tree where he first called me exotic and regaled me with stories of what life would hold for us when we completed our degrees.

His dreams did not include short cuts. He wanted to experience it all, and he was willing to work hard to make it happen. That, and the fact that he wanted a big family, made me see him in a different light than other guys I'd met.

The young girl that I was enjoyed the conversations talking about our futures and soon we were an item.

Loving John came easy. When we were finally married, the most important part of the ceremony was, "Do you promise to love, honor and cherish… through sickness and through health… till death do you part?" When I responded, my answer was engraved in my heart. That's what my marriage meant to me. I became his wife and helpmate; he became my husband, my provider, my protector. He was the king to my queen. He treated me as my father would have wanted him to. He gave me a home. I gave him babies to fill it with. We gave them lots of love. The stuff a good marriage is made of.

CHAPTER 3

White sandy beaches in Tahiti drew us to the oceanfront. Walking barefoot in the tropical morning light, we were like teenagers. We were celebrating John's fortieth birthday. It wasn't often that we were able to get away from the hustle and bustle of our lives to spend some time together. While we had a built-in-babysitter in Ma Wiley, John's mother, and Zita, John's godmother, we didn't like to leave the children for long periods of time.

Before we were married and John had more promises than money, he'd promised to take me someplace exotic every year. This trip to Tahiti was the most romantic thing he could have possibly done. It made me feel that after all this time, he was still excited about our marriage and it made me love him more.

On this island paradise, we reconnected over food, tropical drinks and late night discussions. The resort and spa where we stayed was top rated and the service was magnificent.

When we vacation together we try to take an experience back home with us. This time we decided to take sailing lessons. The weather was its usual year-round perfect with just enough of a wind to make lessons doable. I had a great time watching John exert himself, yelling "ahoy mate" every time he actually did something right. I didn't want to dampen his ardor by telling him that he was not a pirate.

The last night, we walked barefoot along the beach holding hands like young lovers. Waves gently lapped the shore as the moon made a silver highway in the water that led to the other side of the world. Noise from a party about a quarter of a mile or so down the beach wafted on a night breeze. As we danced to the rhythm in our heads, I had never been happier

The next day we headed back to the real world on a flight which would take us first to Hawaii and then on to Houston. Totally satiated and drowsy, we claimed our seats and fell asleep almost before the plane taxied down the runway.

CHAPTER 4

Tired and still sleepy from our flight back to Houston, we presented ourselves at customs to be allowed to enter the States and to declare our gifts. Like the tourists we were, we had bought gifts for everybody. Neither of us thought much of it when the customs agent looked at our passports and back at us as though we were trying to sneak the Hope Diamond into the country. The man was just doing his job, I thought.

It was more than an overzealous agent. It was the long arm of the law. Without much of a warning, John was taken into custody. I was now fully awake and pressed the officers for as much detail as possible. John was being made to look like a criminal with his hands behind his back with cuffs lacing them together.

"Baby, call the attorney, he will know what to do. His number is in your phone", John said as he issued orders for me to follow as they led him away.

I have never thought of myself as a person that springs into action. I have always been a thinker. I mull things over. But that day, I began to get a different idea of how to respond when someone you love is threatened.

Digging into my purse, I struggled to remember the name of the attorney John and I had spoken with prior to going on our trip. I had to dial a couple of times because he did not answer on the first couple of rings. The hands on the clock ticked in slow motion as the attorney advised me on what to do while he flew to Hawaii to be with me and to bail my husband out of jail.

I secured lodging at a local hotel in Honolulu and began to wait for I knew not what and to rack my brain about what I knew for a fact and what I suspected. The hotel was absolutely beautiful but I barely saw the lavish décor in the lobby. Although the hotel staff did not know me from any other guest, my imagination worked overtime. Surely everybody must know what was happening in my life. When the front desk clerk requested identification, momentarily I was confused about whether to give him my driver's license or my passport. Finally, I settled on my driver's license but could not look the clerk in the eye. Circumstance has a way of quickly reducing your status.

With John in jail, I somehow felt like I was the prisoner in that magnificently designed suite. It took room service fifteen short minutes to bring me a pot of hot kiwi and strawberry tea. I started the jets in the Jacuzzi then attempted to soak the weariness from my bones and relax enough to have merciful sleep. Sipping tea, I eased myself lower into the water. The scent of Jasmine hung heavy in the air.

I may as well have been on a rollercoaster. My wired mind did not respond to this gentle treatment.

Hot tea and a hot bath and I was still wide awake. No matter how I fitted my body on those cool white sheets, sleep eluded me. We should have been on a flight headed back to Houston to our children. Instead, it was left up to me to explain the situation to Ma Wiley and she would have the responsibility of explaining to the children why we'd be late getting back home.

Daylight found me no closer to an answer that would satisfy the questions in my head than I was with the first cup of tea. I was certain of one thing only. John and I were more than a couple; we were a team in the many ways that count. I'd be in his corner through thick and thin.

CHAPTER 5

As soon as the time difference would allow me to call my best friend, Jackie, without rousing her entire household, I dialed her number. The minute I heard her voice, I blurted out the news. Jackie was a friend to both John and me. She had been listening to my tales of woe since the days when we were in college. Sounding like a school alarm, she admonished me to slow down, take my time and tell her what was happening. I continued to rush in an effort to have her understand that John had been arrested and that I was in Honolulu holed up in a hotel waiting for the attorney to come and bail John out.

This was the first time I had mentioned our troubles to anyone outside of the immediate family. As I explained to Jackie, shame began to ease itself into my conversation. At the very time that we were beginning the first round of a fight not of our choosing, I was flooded with the stigma of shame. Even though I knew we were not the kind of people who ended up in jail because we didn't do the things that criminals did, I asked Jackie not to mention this to anybody else. She understood my dilemma as I knew she would.

I had not called Jackie for advice but she always gave it whether you asked for it or not. She said now was the time for me to take a look at how John and I had gotten to where we were in life and try to figure out what that meant to me. She promised the answers would come when I looked in the right place.

CHAPTER 6

From the moment John and I started to seriously date back in college, we had mapped out where we wanted our careers to go and how we planned on getting there. We made and honored our vows. We made all of the important decisions together: when to have children and how to discipline them, where and when to buy a house, how to save and invest our money, where to vacation, that we would vote for whomever we chose without fear of cancelling out the other's vote. And little things from not eating red meat more than twice a week to what movie we should see at the theater.

He believed in me and I believed in him. Now I was faced with one of two choices, either believe my husband when he told me he'd done nothing wrong, or to believe what others had to say about him.

My choice was simple; I not only believed my husband, I believed in my husband. I believed he would do nothing to jeopardize his freedom or my life and the lives of our children. He knew everything he did reflected on the entire family. I believed he was caught up in a sting that took as gospel the word of people willing to sacrifice him so that they could retain their own freedom.

I kept at this line of thinking until the attorney arrived in Honolulu to bail John out of jail. While we were celebrating John's birthday on white sandy beaches in Tahiti, a Federal Grand Jury sitting in the Houston Division of the Southern

District of Texas returned an indictment which included 121 counts against my husband and nearly a dozen other pharmacists. The indictment was almost guaranteed when a handful of people including a physician, exchanged their testimony for a more lenient sentence, admitting their culpability and pointing a deadly finger at my husband. This action had the desired effect for the government's prosecuting attorney and John and his business partner were pursued straight into court.

The attorney and I headed to the Honolulu department of corrections and on the way, I resigned myself to the journey that lay ahead. I knew John and I would fight these allegations with everything we had and I would be by his side. It was important for me to let him know that I would always support him.

CHAPTER 7

This was the culmination of an investigation into alleged improprieties in a pharmacy owned by John and his business partner. The Federal Government had accused the two of them of, in essence, becoming "street" drug dealers. What they said was "conspiracy to distribute illegal narcotics." What they meant was "street drug dealer." At the core of the government's allegations was the sale of physician prescribed narcotics in the form of millions of pills and gallons of liquid.

John was not the only pharmacist targeted for this investigation. We had heard rumbling of a full-scale investigation being conducted into the business dealings of eight or nine local area pharmacists. Still, when John and I discussed this investigation, he assured me he had nothing to be overly concerned about. His business was above board and could stand any amount of scrutiny the government wanted to give.

Knowing this was a federal investigation, I insisted that we talk with an attorney to see what our options were. We sought the counsel of one of John's friends who suggested another attorney more skilled with these types of cases. John believed he had done nothing wrong and I believed in him. He was very vocal and adamant about his innocence and made the decision to continue his business activities and went to work at the pharmacy every day while the investigation was waged.

Things seemed to be progressing rather nicely and months passed without a mention of findings from an audit of John's pharmacy and prescription records. Secure in this knowledge, John and I planned a mini vacation at the end of the month. He'd be celebrating his fortieth birthday. I had done the research on Tahiti and over dinner, presented him with brochures to get him in the mood.

We spent one glorious week in Tahiti rejuvenating in the sun; strengthening our marriage and having all kinds of fun. I wrapped myself in the thought that I felt like a new bride. We worked at bringing and keeping romance in our marriage and this time it paid off in spades.

I'd like to think we still would have spent that time together had we known it would be the end of happiness as we knew it. Especially if we had known. But, we didn't have a clue.

CHAPTER 8

We sat on hard polished benches in the federal courtroom on the 14th floor, holding hands and straining to hear opening arguments. My only taste of courtroom drama had been served up by Johnnie Cochran. I, like all of America, watched as Johnnie proclaimed "If it don't fit, you must acquit." This was proving to be a trial of the same magnitude. My husband and his business partner were on trial fighting for their very existence. Twelve people sat in the jury box to the left of the judge's bench facing a side view of the defendants and their high-powered lawyers.

The first day at trial, I arrived earlier than the actual court time because I was on edge and very close to having an anxiety attack. I was there when John entered the courtroom and I mentally checked his appearance. He had not been allowed to come home since being arrested, so the day before and each day thereafter, I selected his entire outfit; suit, shirt, tie, shoes, socks, and lucky underwear so he would not look like a prisoner in the traditional orange prison jumpsuit.

He looked good, slightly worried but good. To his credit, he'd lost five pounds or so. His eyes were bright and his skin had a deep current of red. He was animated while talking with his lawyers. This became the customary routine for me, selecting clothing each day to be delivered to the jail so he'd appear normal before the jury.

We made eye contact and I smiled and made a circle with my fingers raising my hand to let him know that things were ok.

He nodded and gave me a smile as well. This small gesture lifted my spirits and I relaxed a bit as I waited for Ma Wiley to join me.

Jackie slid into the bench with me and grabbed my hand. She had beaten Ma Wiley by a few minutes. As we hugged, she whispered that everything was going to be alright. I needed her to tell it to me over and over again because I desperately wanted to believe her. At the speed of which things were progressing, I was beginning to have serious doubts.

Minutes later, Ma Wiley arrived and quietly joined us. John was an only-child and much loved by his mom. She vowed not to miss a day of the trial, and she lived up to that promise. She was right there with me every step of the way to watch proceedings, closely looking for anything that would help John's defense.

Ma Wiley and I created quite a picture each day as we sat patiently waiting for proceedings to begin. One or the other of us would take notes and we'd pour over them after the day's end looking for inconsistencies in the prosecutor's case. The court may have a verbatim transcript of the proceedings but they did not share them with us.

The courtroom was filled with other defendants' families and friends and a handful of law school students trying to get a first hand view of real court room theatrics. This was a high profile case that involved many professional men with standing in the community so the balance of the seating in the courtroom was filled with spectators and media types.

I appreciated the fact that Jackie came as often as possible. I wanted her there. I could bounce things off of her and she could give me candid responses. Something, anything to help John.

A live trial has no resemblance to a made-for-TV movie. For one thing, time is not your friend. Nobody is in a hurry and things move at a snail's pace. With free time to mull things over, I began to worry about what would happen to the kids and me if John was found guilty.

As parents, we had made the decision to not involve the children in something so life altering as the possibility of prison. I tried to push these negative thoughts from my mind, but you can't sit in court each day and listen to the evidence and walk away unscathed. I believe that's why the law states beyond a reasonable doubt. It's reasonable to be swayed when you hear the same thing over and over again.

The trial ran for thirteen exceptionally long days before the jury was sent to deliberate John's future. Five days later, they still had not reached a verdict. At least one juror had reasonable doubt which was sufficient for the judge to declare a mistrial due to a hung jury.

During times of great stress, the mind can play tricks and it may become nearly impossible to tell the difference from what you hear and what you think you hear. What I heard was "hung jury." I was so excited about the results that I translated "hung jury" to mean "not guilty."

CHAPTER 9

Joy does not describe how I felt. Picking up the phone, I ordered dinner for twenty-five that included brisket Texas style, and country smoked sausage baked beans, and potato salad with all the trimmings, to be picked up from John's favorite place. I then ran by the local grocer to pick up a German chocolate cake. He hadn't had a decent meal since he went to jail and I was determined to feed him all of his favorite foods.

What a celebration! Ma Wiley and Jackie and a couple of the few friends that remained by our side met at the house to welcome John home. With the hyper media coverage of the trial, many in our circle of friends had turned their backs on us, leaving us to sink or swim alone. The number would pare itself down to a bare minimum as the spectacle of our lives continued to unfold.

John and I were regular members at the largest church in the Houston area where the goodness of God and His mercy were the mainstay of its leader. I had not expected my pastor and members from his congregation to shun us, but they did. Although we were not in church each time the doors opened, we were there frequently. We contributed to a ministry that we believed in, we paid our tithes and offerings, and we participated in the church family. Finding ourselves on the wrong end of a federal investigation, we asked for an audience with the pastor for counseling. I was left speechless when told that he would not see us. I was stunned and more than a little hurt that not a one person from the church was there to celebrate with us.

John's homecoming party was an event of love. By now we had three children and they missed their father as was evident by the three of them nearly pasting themselves to his side. If he sat, a child was on his lap and one was between his legs. The other was hanging on to his neck. The thrill of being able to touch him. Their daddy was home! Ma Wiley literally floated through the house doting on her precious child. Her entire conversation commenced with either "can I get you" or "do you want some more of."

All the while John was in jail, those people that remained friends with the family constantly prayed for us. They became mighty warriors, praying until something broke the hold on my family. Offended by the mega church where we belonged, I sought another church where I could worship and feel in the presence of God. I read my Bible and constantly looked for Scripture to help me understand what was going on in my life. I prayed as best I could and beseeched God to show me the right way to go. Celebrating his release from jail was very special. Among other things, it meant that God had answered our prayers.

CHAPTER 10

Jackie was President of a very well respected campus organization. I was a freshman pharmacy student looking for a place to belong. Never in my life had I been so alone. My family had lived a quiet life in Canada and although it hurt me to leave them, I made the decision to come to the States to study. Dad wasn't happy about letting me go but he knew it was time for me to spread my wings.

By the time I met Jackie, my wings were still tucked beneath my body. I was either stuck in my room or at the library or sitting under a tree filling my head with Anatomy and Physiology, Biology, or Pharmacology determined to get grades that would qualify me for a scholarship. Jackie, on the other hand, had a life. She was not only an upperclassman in pharmacy school, she was involved in everything. She recruited me to join her organization and actually hung around to make sure I made a few friends and experienced a little campus life.

One Friday night Jackie invited me to go to the Hunan Buffet located a couple of miles from campus. She literally saved my life. I had been practically living on Ramen Noodles and cold cereals, and not all of the time with milk. Spread before us in this establishment was all of the food I could eat for the princely price of $7.95 plus tax and a very tiny tip. At least once a month we went out to dinner taking full advantage of the budget buffet. I hope the wait staff understood that we had absolutely no money.

For that reason alone, when I dine out, I now over-tip the wait-staff and if the meal has been especially good, I send my compliments to the chef.

Jackie was a people person and was always with a group of people fighting a cause or bringing people together. She was a natural born leader. Over our regular dinners, we got to know each other. She had a genuine interest in everything about me. A genuine interest in where I was from, our culture. We'd talk for hours about what life was like in Trinidad and Canada.

Then, she introduced me to her Houston. American football, free concerts, the mall, craw fish (mud bugs she called them), brisket without Bar-B-Q sauce, and Maize. Then there was the Blues, Houston style.

To this day, I don't remember the details, I think there was a vote, but to my surprise, I was named Homecoming Queen, selected from Jackie's organization. Jackie said she had nothing to do with it, but I didn't believe her. I was filled with as much dread as excitement. Excitement because what girl doesn't want to be a queen for once in her life. I had never dreamed I would have that kind of attention except on my wedding day. Dread because I had nothing decent to wear. I couldn't afford a meal most of the time. Surely, I couldn't afford a dress and the whole nine yards that went with being Homecoming Queen.

When I told Jackie why I couldn't possibly accept, she wouldn't hear it. Proclaiming me already a queen, she immediately dragged me to her place in search of a dress befitting my new-found royal status. We went through everything in her closets until we located a dress that called my name when I tried it on. It was exquisite. Had I not known differently, I would have thought it was tailor made just for me. Somehow I got shoes and a clutch bag to match and the queen thing began to fall into place.

The day of the big game, Jackie treated us to a manicure and pedicure which she paid for with a buy one, get one free coupon after which she styled my hair and applied my make-up. Never has there been a Homecoming Queen that looked better or felt better about herself than I did on that day, thanks to Jackie. That was her way. She made people bigger and better just by being their friend. She became my champion, the person with whom I shared the events of my life and she kept an eye out for me as my wings began to unfold.

When Jackie graduated, she went to work as a pharmacist for a large chain and moved on with her life. I stayed behind, comfortable in my little world, working my plan and trying to find my place, my reason for being.

CHAPTER 11

Part of finding my place led me to John. We just sort of clicked. They, those people responsible for handing down folk lore, say that when love comes you will both know it. It did not come as much as it grew between us. We enjoyed each other's company. I took him to the Hunan Buffet. Who could not fall in love with me over a fifty-five item menu that also included Sushi?

He was a man after my own heart, a strong man like I remembered my father being. Turns out, we had more in common than school. He wanted to be a father with lots of children. Being an only child, he had yearned for brothers and sisters for years. Having a large family would help to fill that emptiness. I sympathized with him because there was only two of us in my family and we were so far apart in age that I felt alone most of the time.

Then as life would have it, Jackie was back. Somewhere along the way, she had met my John and she introduced him to the world of finance by way of an investment club. Just as she had been a guiding light for me in the early days, now, she became a beacon to John. They made money together.

Later, John and I were married with Jackie right there for the both of us. She fitted the veil over my face and just for the heck of it, sat me down to explain what would happen on my wedding night. We laughed so hard I got hiccups listening to her explain the birds and bees and honey. Once again, she had done what she set out to do; make me feel at ease on the most important day of my life.

I've searched for appropriate words to describe how John and I felt about marriage. "Together" seems to spell it out. I wanted lots of children, sixteen to be exact. He was more practical; two boys and two girls would do it for him. We both wanted a home filled with love, and happiness, extended family, real and adopted. We wanted to travel and enjoy the fruit of our labor. He wanted to show me the world, and I wanted to see it with him. We were willing to work hard for the things we desired.

After watching John and I pledge our lives together, Jackie was in my space more and more and our friendship was fully rekindled. Time passed and life was good for both of us. We saw each other as regularly as possible. Since Jackie was the first to get married, it was only fitting that she was the first to have a baby. She had already charted the course and perfected things with a second baby by the time I had my strapping baby boy. I was finally on the road to raising my much wanted large family.

Jackie became the big sister that I'd never had. She helped me to become not just a mother but a mom. All I had to do was emulate her. I thought she was the best mother ever. She just seemed to know what to do at any given moment. Funny how she knew all about kids and all about loving and giving, but married a man who seemed to have been born without that gene altogether.

Although the four of us spent much time together, I didn't really like her husband. I thought she deserved better. He never seemed to be putting as much energy into her and their family as she did. He was more standoffish and cool, the very opposite of the loving and giving woman that he had married. She loved him with everything that was in her and seemed blind to his faults.

As much as I wanted to grab her and shake some sense into her head, the more I knew I should keep my place. Jackie saw the good in everybody and nothing I said would change who and what she was. Instead of criticizing her choice of mate, I chose to just be her friend.

John and Jackie's husband were able to bond somewhat and if he were telling the tale, he would say John was his best friend. It was on such a note that we began to take our vacations together.

One year, we decided to go to Spain. This was our first international vacation as married couples and we decided to wing it. Instead of planned tours, we decided to strike out on our own with travel brochures and maps and see some of the country for ourselves. Early mornings found us out in the fresh air, strolling through the marketplace sampling wares. The food was incredibly good and the people were wonderful to Americans. We discovered museums to rival the great museums of the world and gardens like none other.

My favorite sights were the many cathedrals. It was as though the architect of one simply tried with all of his might to outdo the others and we spent a lot of time looking at these monuments to a people's faith. We spent our evenings dancing and listening to music, our heads filled with all we'd seen and done during the day. Near the end of our vacation, we took a day-trip to Morocco which turned out to be less than one hundred miles from Spain. We were perfect tourists.

This trip served to strengthen our relationship with Jackie and her husband and brought us closer together as a family. In fact, I believe I conceived our second child, Jason, on this awe inspired trip. Even though my pregnancy was marred with prenatal concerns and I needed constant rest and medical attention, nearly nine months to the day, we delivered another healthy baby boy into the world. Life was indeed good and our little family was growing. As God would have it, not long after, we welcomed a beautiful baby girl

With the new baby, my days grew longer, my nights shorter, and my patience thinner but I coped. Notice I did not say I coped well. Three children, a husband and a job were beginning to take a toll. John was paying more attention to the stress I was under and we discussed what our alternatives were. Somewhere in the middle of the night, we hit upon the idea that I should quit work and become a stay at home mom.

As I got a little free time to spend with Jackie, I learned she'd been diagnosed with breast cancer. Jackie drifted as she processed what was happening to her body. I used the word processed because that's what she always said… "I'm processing this". The process led to a double mastectomy and chemotherapy. As expected, she lost her hair, she lost weight, she had no appetite and she was always tired. There were days when she could barely put one foot in front of the other.

Life is a continuous learning process and that's when I learned how to love and I learned how to pray. It's at times like these when nothing matters because no amount of anything you have will take this sickness away. And still we prayed. Her children needed their mother, scarred and imperfect, baby-fine hair and all, and finally she began to turn the corner. Her coloring returned and ten extra pounds on her frame made her look good. Doctors gave her a clean bill of health and we began to count down the five years when doctors would proclaim her healed.

All while it was touch-n-go for Jackie, I shopped with a purpose. The people at the wig shop knew me on sight. I bought wigs to make her laugh and to make her look good. Wanting her to experience some fun, I presented her with an "Annie" wig and a "Marilyn Monroe" wig, along with a short "Afro" and a long "Dreadlock" wig. We sat looking in the mirror and sang off key as much of the hit soundtrack song "Tomorrow," as we could remember.

I shopped for lingerie. The works. Matching sets with padding to make her feel beautiful while she waited to be properly fitted. Night gowns, bed jackets, robes. Most of the time she was not feeling up to accompanying me into the wilds of the mall, so I hauled packages to her and we played dress-up.

I'd like to think that Jackie's husband did not know how to cope with her illness and the imperfections in the aftermath. While he had always been somewhat chilly, he became more withdrawn to the point of almost being cold. He could not or would not look at her nude body. While he never appeared to be an affectionate man, he withdrew completely and Jackie was not only devastated by the cancer but by the inconsideration of her husband.

Finding an out for her husband's rejection, Jackie focused on the love of her children and became a super mom. She channeled his rejection into as much love for everybody that surrounded her as she could muster. Not only was she battling a disease that wins more often than not, it now appeared she'd be heading for divorce court.

Her loss became my loss, her pain of divorcing her husband became my pain. We became sister girls. She taught me about grace under pressure, how to fight, how to heal and how to never give up. She wasn't a quitter and I learned these lessons well. More importantly, she taught me the meaning of selfless love for your children. Although I did not realize it at the time, she taught me the importance of being a stable, positive force for my children, that no matter what happened to me, they should be my reason for everything.

CHAPTER 12

With John back at home, my primary function was to bring my family back on track as quickly as possible. John headed back to the pharmacy and I resumed my role as stay at home mom with a vengeance. I cooked and cleaned and sometimes found myself just sitting with a child on my lap, hugging one or the other of them nestled to my body. I was crazy happy. While cleaning the house, I sang loud enough for the entire neighborhood to hear me and I danced with wild abandonment. I conjured up every dance I'd ever learned and a few which had not been invented at the time.

No matter what time John arrived home in the evening, I'd fly into his arms never wanting again to be denied the opportunity. In my truly alone moments, I thanked God for giving me back my family. I tried to bargain, promising to become the best person I could be to prove how much I appreciated God sending John back home to us. The children and John prospered under my watchful eye.

John was as attentive to the family as I had become and was normally home by nine every night. It had rained all day, at first great fat raindrops that soaked everything in its path then later turned into fine stinging water that pierced the spirit and called for chicken soup. I answered the call with chicken soup and for good measure, threw in some of my handmade fluffy dumplings. On this particular night, John arrived home early and appeared preoccupied with something. I figured we'd talk about it after I put the children down for the night.

Sitting on his lap, comfortable just being so close to him, I listened as he began to map out new developments of the case against him. John had been advised by his counsel that the government would likely try the case again. He went on to explain what this meant to him but I could not buy into what he was saying. In my mind that was a physical impossibility. I told myself that my husband was a free man in every sense of the word and he was going to stay a free man. I remained on his lap but I was not feeling what he was trying to tell me. Even then I was busy developing a one-sided view of my surroundings.

I had no history with the criminal justice system. Everything that I knew or suspected came from television shows like Judge Judy and Judge Mathis with a smattering of CSI-SVU thrown in. Television had not been of interest to me beyond special events. I watched the Olympic Games, The Final Four (not The Road to the Final Four) because I had an affinity for college basketball, and *Sixty Minutes*. I had neither the time nor the inclination to sit for hours mindlessly staring at the screen and missing out on real life.

Neither John nor I were street-wise, and while we had the best attorneys we could possibly afford, we had to trust their counsel. Quietly and behind the scenes, his lawyers began to prepare for a second trial. They met frequently to strategize, bounce ideas around, and to try to discover anything which could be used to help John should a second trial become a reality.

At first I had tried to be a part of the solution but I was of no help. I could not believe the government was so blind that they could not see John's innocence. Ultimately, I viewed strategizing as a big waste of time, like preparing for war in time of peace.

John made a big effort at trying to set a survival plan into motion while he could. He wanted me to be prepared just in case. He explained the breakdown of our assets including the house, the business, and the corporate accounts. His attorney had assured him that the government would not touch our individual personal accounts; that this only had to do with the business. John and I discussed what I should do with the remaining money. His advice was that I should pay off as many bills as I could, and estimate what the utilities would cost for a year along with how much money I would need for food and upkeep on my car and insurances and such for a full year, at least.

If necessary, there should be enough money to take care of our family until I commenced work. Then there was the money from my own personal account. He promised the help of Ma Wiley and Zita, which he had no earthly right to do. John's words to me were to be strong in the event things were to go south.

He must have had a premonition. I simply would not listen. I could not buy into what John was trying to tell me. How on earth would I make it if things took another turn and went south?

CHAPTER 13

Five weeks later, peace was over and the second trial began. I immediately went into prayer as did my prayer warriors. I began to fast and pray and once again, called my close-knit friends and asked for their prayers. I knew that God was there, and I knew that he would work a miracle for John and me. After all, he would not have saved John at the end of the first trial just to walk away from him now. I was not grounded in my faith, but I believed.

The thing that I noticed immediately in the courtroom was the jury. This time around, I had a better respect for the jury and what they were capable of as it related to my husband. Instead of wondering how they viewed my husband's physical appearance, I worried about how they judged his character and integrity. Had his attorneys proven their case beyond a reasonable doubt?

I scrutinized every member of the jury with a fine eye trying to decipher body language. What did the slight nod of the head of one person mean? Did the fact that one juror starred constantly at John mean we could count on him to favor the defendant or the prosecution? Did the fact that I was there every day hurt or help John? What about Ma Wiley? Did they notice her and was her misery evident to them?

Finding it difficult to balance my faith with what was going on in the natural, I was nearly out of my mind with fear and I harbored a secret that would become highly apparent soon if I did not tell John.

I was pregnant! How could I tell John? He had more on his plate than any one person should have to handle. I should have told him as soon as I knew for sure. We could have shared in the joy of having this child as we did the others, except I was waiting for the perfect time to shower him with good news. I missed my moment.

John would be happy when I told him I was pregnant, because babies were in our plan, and lots of them, but he also knew I always had complications. He knew that I was always at high risk and he'd worry about me and the baby night and day. We couldn't afford the distraction that unnecessary worry would cause. I was counting on this second trial to be as speedy as the first and that John would be home for good before I had to explain the thickness in my mid-section.

Even though John was free and came home each day during this trial, I was a wreck. As I see it now, I was just the opposite of what I portrayed during the first trial. All of my faith was seeping out. During the first trial, I was certain my husband would be found innocent if only the jury understood what was really going on. And when the reality of that trial was over, I let my defenses down. Now, I was almost paralyzed with fear. Although I was in the courtroom, I found my attention span just was not what it had been during the first trial. I conjured up every bad thing possible.

As my body overflowed with hormones and the baby grew inside me, I feared being manic depressive. There were times when I was euphoric about another baby, someone to hold and someone to hold on to me. Someone to give me a reason for pretending to live. At other times, I could picture myself having to raise four children alone.

I had to get a stronger grip on reality. Feeling the time would never be perfect to shower John with the good news that I was pregnant, I decided to tell him one evening after dinner. Pulling me to him, my face buried in the hollow of his neck, we finally celebrated this new Wiley baby.

CHAPTER 14

I had not missed a day in court, yet I was so thoroughly involved in playing "what if," I missed hours at a time of testimony and failed to get a clue of how the trial was going. By the time my thoughts were reigned in, I could not fully appreciate the mounting evidence against John. Clearly the prosecution had done its job.

"We, the jury, find the defendant, John Wiley, guilty ..." I could not hear. I thought I was deaf. The jury foreman's lips continued to move but nothing was registering. The first sound I heard was a guttural moan coming from behind me. It moved into my throat and I could not seem to inhale. I struggled to catch my breath and as I tried to push the air from my lungs, it made the sound of someone suffering from sleep apnea. The cross between a snore, a moan, and gasp for air was my life crashing to the ground.

That was the sound of justice being denied. I turned to Ma Wiley to see what was happening. She stood looking at me with eyes that did not blink and put her finger to her lips and pulled me to her bosom. "Shish, baby, please don't." I felt my insides about to burst. The content of my stomach rose and threatened to spill from between my lips. I swallowed hard, pushing it back down. I heard her every word twice as loud as she normally spoke.

"Did you hear that?" I asked. "Did you hear him say that John was guilty? Who are these people? Did they hear the same evidence that I heard?" I was in stage two of shock, gasping for air and unable to comprehend what was happening, unable to function.

My eyes found John's and communicated without speaking as we had done since the beginning of our relationship. Not paying attention to anything else going on at the moment, he looked into my eyes and knew exactly what I was feeling. He helped me get control of myself. Without taking his eyes away, he inhaled deeply allowing his chest to rise and expand and I did the same following his lead. He pushed his shoulders back and squared his jaw and a second later, I followed suit.

To show his approval, he let me know with a quick nod that I was doing fine. I mouthed my affection for him in words we both understood. "I love you." He held me in his eyes a second longer then turned his attention to the matter at hand.

In that moment before he was led from the courtroom by the bailiff with his attorney in tow, a lifetime of pain and sorrow passed between us. My heart reached out to him. Our course had been set by the jury and that was the hand we would have to play from this moment forward.

Today, he would not be coming home with me. He would not be coming back to say his goodbyes to the children. He was now and for all times, a convicted criminal. For the rest of our lives, he would be labeled a criminal and the world would not care if he actually committed a crime or not. The jury had spoken.

I heard the hollow thud the Judge's gavel made as he tried to silence the crowd. Wives and family members and general spectators were all talking and crying at one time. The sound of that gavel chilled me to the bone and I turned with Ma Wiley and Zita and stumbled from the courtroom. Less than ten steps down the hallway, I called Jackie. Finding humor where none existed, she quipped that now he would have to shelve his run for the presidency.

CHAPTER 15

Jackie had always been whoever I needed her to be depending on the circumstances. She had been my gift, my friend, my sister, my sister-girl, and this day, she became my other mother.

She arrived at Ma Wiley's house shortly after we did. Sweeping in the door, we embraced. We cried together and she prayed. I could not. During the previous months, I had talked to God, I had begged God, I had tried to bargain with God and He had not listened to anything I had to say. Jackie's words were simple, she thanked God for being with us during this time and for seeing us safely through. She asked for guidance and strength to carry on. Then, she prayed for my unborn baby. I was now nearly five months pregnant.

Leaving Ma Wiley's house, I went home to be with my children. I had to tell them something even if it was only that their dad would not be home that night. Children are almost always more resilient than we give them credit for. They were asleep shortly after I got them to bed.

I sat in the rocking chair surrounded by the darkness of our family room, holding a glass of whiskey with both hands as I balanced it on my protruding belly. For the first time in my life, I needed a drink. I needed to feel the alcohol burn my throat. Maybe the burn would outweigh the pain. I held the glass under my nose and sucked in the aroma. Silent tears cascaded into my bosom as I swirled the alcohol around and around. Summoning all of my courage, I flung the glass against the wall and watched the contents make a mess with shattered glass on the floor.

I couldn't even get relief with a stiff drink. I was pregnant and as much as I wanted to take that drink, I wanted not to hurt my baby more. Yet the pull of the alcohol was so great that I called Jackie to talk me down. That night, we won the alcohol battle.

I don't really know how I managed from the day of the verdict to the day of sentencing, but in that short span of time, five or six weeks, things got worse for John and as a consequence, much worse for those of us left at home.

When I was able to pray, I repeatedly asked God to move the Judge's heart to view John's entire record prior to sentencing. John had never been in trouble. He was an honest man. He tried to do the right thing. He was a good husband and an excellent father. He was an only child and was good to his mother. He went to church. He donated his time and money to charities, to schools. That should have counted for something.

I was believing God for the judge to be lenient with his sentencing. I simply moved from one set of begging prayers to the next. I prayed and asked everybody else to pray. But no matter how much I prayed, the government was not done with John. At sentencing, Ma Wiley and I again sat quietly together, she holding my hand, me absentmindedly rubbing her thigh.

Being in court on a regular basis gave me a genuine appreciation for television. I was amazed at how slow things are done in the real world. They seem to take a perverted pleasure in dragging things out ad nauseam. The judge took his own sweet time entering the courtroom. In response to the bailiff's summons, we all stood out of respect for the judge, then attorneys started to approach the bench. It took forever, and finally after what seemed hours, he was ready to finish leveling my life.

I could not hear what John's attorney said to the judge nor what the prosecuting attorney said. However, the judge responded in words something to the effect that standing before him was a very smart, even brilliant man who had taken a wrong turn in life. He said he was convinced of his guilt and equally as convinced about his lack of remorse. He went on to say more mean and hateful things about John and ended his diatribe with the fact that there would be no probation from his courtroom. That said, he then sentenced John to ten years in Federal Prison on the charges he was brought up on.

Not nearly done with the sentencing, the judge quickly issued a decree of forfeiture, ordering us to vacate our home, and seizing John's bank accounts and other assets.

Clearly, I must not have been paying attention when the attorneys told us of the possibility of forfeiture. I now had almost total recall. I could hear the attorney explaining that if John was found guilty, the government would try to take everything they thought was bought with money earned as a result of committing a particular crime. Our home now qualified as ill gotten gain.

At that moment, it struck me that I should not lie down and play dead. The government had taken my husband and torn my family to bits and pieces, but I had no intentions of letting them take my house. John and I had worked for home ownership. In the beginning, I worked to earn money to buy the things we wanted and my money helped to buy that house. If it took getting another lawyer to fight for my right to keep my house, then I'd happily spend every dime I had.

Earlier in the morning, I had walked into that courtroom a pregnant mother and a wife with a house and cars, some money in the bank, with many of the trappings that go with hard work and sacrifice. I walked out a married single mother. In four short months, I would deliver a baby that would be ten years old before he saw his dad from behind bars.

Bitter? Heck yes! Broken? Never!

CHAPTER 16

To say that I was angry would be an understatement.
I was stark raving mad and nothing or nobody could help me.
For once, I was tired of praying to a God who paid no attention
to me. I was nine months pregnant with a baby that I called
my hope and real hope had walked out on me months ago. I
needed somebody or something to help assuage this pain. If it
were possible, I would have just disappeared into thin air. But I
couldn't. I had major responsibilities.

Even though my world was crumbling down around my
feet, and my emotions were all over the place. Having no other
outlet, I continued to make a weak effort at going to church and
getting some strength from hearing the gospel. After the second
trial, I wallowed in shame and self pity and cut myself off
further from most of the people I knew. Except for Ma Wiley,
Zita, and Jackie, I saw one or two of the other wives with
husbands who were also embroiled in the same battle as John.

Not wanting to deal with the stares and unasked
questions of an entire congregation, I began to get most of
my "church" from TV ministries. That's where I made the
acquaintance of a most charismatic minister that held me
spellbound.

Pastor Bridget Fominyam Israel was being interviewed
by someone on television, the name of whom I've forgotten,
and with her was a gentleman named Prophet Cure. She
insisted on being called Pastor Bridget, I suspect, because her

last name was difficult for the average person to pronounce. She talked about the power of prayer and deliverance. As I listened, her voice became a living force and fairly crackled like thunder and lightning. I had never heard a voice quite like that, so spirit filled.

This woman had a real anointing and I sat riveted in that spot, on that day, and began to understand the substance of life. She spoke her sermon directly to me and at that moment, my heart was opened to receive. She mesmerized me with what she said as much as how she said it. On many occasions, I had heard pastors deliver the same message, yet I never made the connection. Could it be that I could not accept the sermon until the need for prayer and deliverance was of a personal nature?

Before the trial, John and I attended church and did the things expected of that congregation. When they refused to give us a consultation after the trouble started, we moved on to a place where we felt more welcomed. My physician's husband was a minister and we periodically worshiped with them. All of that movement, yet we had not branched out or moved outside of our spiritual comfort zone until our troubles took us in a new direction.

My thinking was that I had tried God and I was now getting the feeling I was not doing something right, but Pastor Bridget explained things at a base level that I had never experienced. The program ended with her inviting the viewing audience to attend a conference where she would also be speaking a few days hence.

Not wanting to go out into public alone, I dragged another defendant's wife with me to the conference. It was held in a strip mall church, not the usual edifice that we were accustomed to attending. This was a first for both of us. I was filled with anticipation and ignited with hope because I believed that at last, God was trying to tell me something. I was ready to hear the Word.

When we arrived we were approximately thirty minutes early and Pastor Bridget was in the middle of prayer with those already in attendance. My heart and soul fit right in. Her prayer seemed to lift to the heavens as she glorified God in the natural and in tongues. So effective and so powerful was her prayer that the room could not contain all of the glory and it seeped into my being.

After the conference, my friend and I quickly discussed meeting with the Pastor to tell her about our collective situations and to get some advice and maybe meet with Prophet Cure. We introduced ourselves and began to share our dilemma. Looking back, I can see we must have been the picture of pathetic souls to her, but she didn't show it. Instead, she invited us both to come again and experience the entire conference. I took her up on the invitation, going back several times and each time I experienced an unspeakable joy.

Although I continued to go to my new church, I felt something tugging at my heart string, pulling me back to Pastor Bridget's church to experience that particular brand of praise.

I saw Pastor Bridget as one with a special anointing, a true vessel of God.

Each night prior to settling in for the night, I pulled out my Bible and began to study and read about deliverance and the power of God. My spirit was seeking solace as much as I believed God was seeking me.

About three weeks later, Pastor Bridget gave me a prophetic word concerning my home. She told me that God was sending an angel to protect me and that I would have a home. Her prophesy resonated deep within me.

CHAPTER 17

Until that point, I had practically given up on the idea
of appealing the judge's decision to confiscate our home.
The investigation of my husband's business affairs had also
triggered an investigation into our personal fortunes as they
related to the business. The judge in the case agreed with
the government's contention that funds had been taken from
the business to pay for the house. They did not take into
consideration that I had also worked and earned a respectable
salary from a firm not associated with John's business. They
refused to consider any financial contribution I had legitimately
made.

Initially, I was angry with the government, the judge,
and any and everybody else that had to do with the destruction
which leveled my world. They had taken my husband, my
sanity, my family unit, and now they wanted my house and
whatever money we had left. This anger spurred me into
quickly deciding to fight to the bitter end to save my house, but
it didn't take long for the fire to die inside of me and I moved
on to the path of least resistance. I consoled myself with the
thought that the house, without my husband in it with us, was
simply that; a house. Not a home.

In the year that John and I had been embroiled with the
two legal battles, sometimes just being in the house became an
awesome burden. Everywhere I turned there were reminders
of my husband. Our home was filled with pictures, a constant

reminder of happier times. He smiled at me from every corner. The two of us together; he and each of our children; he with his mother. Our family albums were centered round him. We had chronicled our life together in a series of books to preserve them so that they would be available for our children at some later date and for us to live out again during our golden years.

His closets were still full of his clothing; shoes stacked neatly in the space provided, slippers sitting on the floor waiting for a man that was not scheduled to return for ten years. His toilet articles were where he'd left them the last time he was in the house. His scent, the cologne he wore, wafted out at me every time I opened the door to our bedroom.

Nights were the worst. I'd lie in our bed, cold now because he was not in it with me, and remember him with an intensity that tore me apart. There were many nights after I put the children to bed that I wept while standing in his closet burying my face in his shirts, grieving because he was not there with me.

I missed my husband and I desperately wanted him back. The loneliness was so deep and I experienced such grief until it felt like John had died, not just been sent to prison. My very being could not tell the difference. Although I wanted him back with me, I could not see him ever coming back. Ten years was a lifetime. So I grieved, and my depression deepened.

Whenever I thought about trying to save the house, I couldn't muster the courage to make the effort. I had begun to dislike lawyers with a passion. His, mine and the governments, and the judge and jury were right up there with the rest of them.

If I chose to fight for the house, the government would fight back and they were formidable opponents. If I wanted to stand a chance at winning an appeal, I'd have to retain another lawyer, the sixth, which had thus far been paid a hefty fee with very little in return.

The thought of having to face the same judge yet again almost made me physically ill. The entire legal system was making a killing off of our misery and I wanted to be done with them.

Jackie and Ma Wiley had a different point of view. They believed it my duty to appeal the decision and retain our home because we had worked for it and because it was my children's right to live in the house that their parents had struggled to buy. They did a good job of convincing me to give it my best shot.

I wondered how much money I was going to have to spend. Would I live to see the day when I was no longer in litigation? I owed it to my children. So, I set out to hire another lawyer, this one in addition to the one that was appealing John's case, and began the tedious process of appealing the government's decision in an attempt to save my house.

Pastor Bridget's prophetic word came at the perfect time and helped to cement the decision to fight to keep the house. I viewed her words as a sign from God that everything was going to work for my good with the appeal.

I developed a certain mindset to see me through this litigation. I had been under the stress of a case not of my choosing in excess of a year and was beginning to grow heavy with the baby inside of me. I tried to limit the damage I could be doing to my unborn child and to sandwich care for my other children into my daily plan.

CHAPTER 18

Losing the appeal for the house took the wind out of my sails. It knocked me for a loop. I didn't see it coming. I believed God and the attorney would save my house. Instead, I was given thirty days to vacate the premises. Thirty days to give my house over to the government. The great American dream house which I had helped to buy and pay for so that we could have a place to live was no longer mine.

Ma Wiley and Jackie were firmly in place to help buffer me from this latest defeat. I had been so convinced my house would not be taken that I neglected to make a contingency plan. Apparently Ma Wiley and Jackie had seen things differently. Whereas I had mindboggling questions concerning where I was suppose to take my children to live, they had solved the issue.

I viewed the situation as the government had taken my husband and in so doing made my children fatherless orphans and now they had taken the very house they lived in and in effect made them homeless as well. Ma Wiley and Jackie viewed the situation as us needing to circle the wagons and set out to locate a rental property that we could have access to comfortably within the next thirty days.

Each day I packed our belongings in anticipation of finding a house to rent. I moved through the process as though in a fog. It was too much and my sanity was tested. I tried to pray for guidance and I believed God did not listen. I cursed John for leaving us in this situation, and he did not hear me. I

was alone in this misery. I'd fought yet another fight that I lost
and each time I lost, I had to give up something. My life was
sort of like playing strip poker. You lose, you take something
off. Well, in this game, I was down to my preverbal underwear.

Instead of being able to vacate the house with grace
and dignity, the injustice of it all settled within me and I could
not let it go. After the thirtieth day, and after I had moved my
family to another location, I continued to go back to the house,
drawn to it like a moth to a flame. A secure lock had been
placed on the front and back doors but I owned this house and I
knew of other ways to get inside.

Night after night I went to my house, climbed through a
window in the back and considered myself at home.

The insanity in me allowed me to defy the courts and
enter a house that was no longer mine. My mind functioned
in one vein only. This was my house and I was not going to
leave. I didn't need a house full of furniture and the thousands
of other things to go inside of it for me to know that I was at
home. I didn't need John or the children there to know that I
was at home. My heart knew that I was at home and the sorrow
of it all drove me to commit this final act of defiance.

I cried a bucket of tears while laying blame at
everybody's feet. Six lawyers that we had paid for, the
unlimited supply of government lawyers that everybody's
tax dollars paid for, a judge, twenty-four jurors in addition to

alternates, all of the co-defendants, liars and thieves all, and later I blamed John and Ma Wiley, Jackie, and God.

I wept for my young family. How long is ten years really? I measured it by my children. My oldest child would sit for the SAT while his dad was in prison. He would try to decide what to choose as a career, he would have his first date, his first dance, his first kiss, his first prom. He would possibly attend his first day of undergraduate classes while his dad was in prison.

The boys, they needed a dad every day. Someone to pattern their lives after. Who would they learn the important things in life from? How would they learn what it really means to be a man: how do they provide for the future, how should they love and respect their mother and grandmother, indeed all women. Who should have their back and attend father and son activities and events? Whose strong arms should hold them when monster's come out at night, or when disappointment comes by day, or when they just need a hug from a man? What do I do now?

My daughter needed to be a daddy's girl. She needed to know she was the most beautiful girl in the world to her daddy so she wouldn't fall for a line from predatory guys later in life. She needed to feel like a princess. How would she know how a man is supposed to treat her if she is denied the right to see her daddy treat her mother with love and respect? Where was she supposed to learn how to be a lady if the gentleman in her life was in prison?

Jackie saved me from myself. She was able to see my rapid decline and spoke to me constantly about the health of my unborn child. She'd say if I was not willing to save myself then I must be willing to save my children and in particular, the baby inside of me. I owed it to my children to be a better mother than I had allowed myself to become. Since the baby I was now carrying was a symbol of hope, she said I should treat hope better. I should want to give this baby the best and healthiest mother in the world.

CHAPTER 19

From the time John was arrested, I began to turn into a recluse, shutting out the few people that actually wanted to be around us. Yet Jackie was the only one I trusted completely, and at times I even tried to push her away.

I didn't have many secrets that I kept from Jackie. We'd been through too much together and she always gave excellent advice. She had an understanding of people and incidents which I still haven't mastered. This time, I'd need more than advice. I'd need her by my side to see me through. It was only natural that she was the first to know about the pregnancy.

It wasn't that I was trying to hide the fact, I was trying to spare John the worry about me and the baby for as long as possible

When I confided this to Jackie she just chuckled and asked if I knew that pregnancy was one of the few things that absolutely can't be hidden. I understood what she was saying and told her it wouldn't be too long. I promised to tell John as soon as he was free.

Her understanding of the situation was much more developed than mine. Over the years, my mind replayed her response whenever I questioned why my husband was convicted. "To be honest with you," she looked me right in the eye as she said, " I don't think he's ever going to be free. Every case I've read about pretty much leads to the same thing.

The feds almost always get their man. They have more money, more time, unlimited resources and the fundamental belief that they are always right. How can he beat that, sweetie? Juries give them what they want because they are human. They believe in their government's ability to fight for truth and justice and who in their right mind would not want to be a part of a little bit of history?"

If this had been about anybody else, I would have probably found some humor in what she said, but it wasn't about somebody else, it was about my husband. That was enough for me to decide to tell John about the new addition to the family before the trial was over.

Now, I found myself a single mother of three, soon to be four children and I was terrified. I wept at the drop of a hat, filled with grief and terror. One recurring theme ran through my head constantly. How am I going to do this? How am I going to survive without him? How am I going to take care of us? I was a licensed pharmacist but I was not a practicing pharmacist.

Looking back, the next few months were a blur. I remember going through the pregnancy. Except for the care of a wonderful doctor who attempted to care for the total of me and the strength and caring spirit of Jackie, the pregnancy may have ended differently.

With each pregnancy, it was necessary for me to have a surgical procedure in order to carry the baby to term. With my clouded judgment, I argued against the surgical procedure. I would later be so ashamed for that decision, knowing that my selfishness could have damaged my unborn baby.

Jackie stepped in to talk some sense into me. She pointed out that if I should lose this baby after having lost John, it would be devastating to me and my family. She further pointed out that if I should lose this baby because of something I failed to do, then, the loss would haunt me for the rest of my life.

I threw nasty words right back at her. I yelled that if anything happened to this baby, it would be God's doing. After all, he was the one in charge of everything.

She wasn't having any of my mouth. She pushed back even harder than before, explaining that God was not in charge. That he had given me options and now I had choices to make. She did not scream she just gave it to me as she saw it, asking if I would do the right thing for this baby or would I take my chances on becoming a murderer.

Her words reached all the way through me and squeezed my insides. I turned away from her, not wanting her to see the fear on my face.

She finished by driving her point home with tired breath.

"Is that what you want? Do nothing, and wait to see what happens, or do something and give the baby a fighting chance? The ball is in your court."

I believe God placed both Jackie and my doctor in my life to save me from self-destruction so that my baby would have a chance at life. I did the only thing I could have a hand in; I chose to have the surgery.

John and I had decided to name him Jaxon, in honor of Jackie.

CHAPTER 20

With Pastor Bridget in my life, I was now getting a better understanding of God and how he works in my life every day. We were at Jackie's house when I decided to share with her some of the things I had been learning. I talked to her about the Holy Spirit and the power of prayer and fasting and its ability to break through barriers. She just went silent on me. I thought it odd because Jackie and I always had meaningful conversations. Good, bad or indifferent, she was always responsive, but not this time.

I was happy about finally getting the message. It had certainly taken long enough. However, the more I talked and the more excited I became, the more I noticed Jackie wasn't sharing in it with me. Instead, she became deadly silent.

I changed in mid-sentence to ask her if anything was wrong. After all the things that had happened, I was developing a sixth sense about these things. I thought the mention of the Holy Spirit and the relationship I was trying to develop with God was making her uncomfortable.

She swallowed before attempting to answer. There was something in her voice that I had not heard in years. It caught in her throat and in that short time, I knew even before she put a voice to it. The cancer was back.

I searched her eyes as she told me that she needed to believe the things I had told her about the power of prayer and fasting because her doctors had confirmed that the cancer was back. She had already begun treatment.

I opened my arms to her and immediately began to pray for God's mercy and a healing for her. During the past couple of years, we'd hugged and consoled each other in this manner more than I'd care to think about. I felt her pain and sadness deeply because I had lost my mother to colon cancer a few years back. I wanted to scream but I couldn't, not now. Jackie needed me to be strong.

Cancer was nothing new to either of us. The first time she was diagnosed with breast cancer the result was that she had a double mastectomy, chemotherapy and radiation and she survived. This time she never mentioned where the cancer had attacked and I did not ask because I knew there was no one place better than the other for it to be. Jackie was in trouble and that was all that mattered.

That evening, I contacted my prayer partners and they contacted even more people. I talked to some of Jackie's friends and before anyone knew exactly how it happened, we had pulled together hundreds of people to pray for Jackie to be healed.

CHAPTER 21

This was the year Jackie would turn forty. She announced that she was going to celebrate her 40th birthday for an entire year. I kidded her that she was about to be over the hill. We laughed almost uncontrollably because she said she thought the hill was when you turned thirty. Not so, I said, that was with the old system. The new system is based on "look like." Therefore, when you turn fifty, that's the new forty. Now that you are forty, you become thirty again. The first time you were thirty, you were just twenty for the second time. I could keep this up until you become a baby again for the second time in nearly a half century.

We knew we were being silly but we didn't care. The only thing that concerned us was that we had found something to laugh about.

Combined, we had been down for so long we were searching for a reason. Jackie got the idea that if she celebrated for an entire year, it would be her way of showing her gratitude to God. It seemed like a good idea to me and I eagerly jumped on her train of thought.

During my alone time, I secretly continued to struggle with my own problems. Loneliness and self doubt were my constant companions and now fear of what tomorrow would bring nearly pushed me over the edge. I questioned God about the meaning of this new cancer in Jackie. Had she not suffered enough? Was there something else we should be doing? Was this attack on Jackie God's way of getting my attention? If so, He had it.

I had suffered and Jackie had suffered more. She'd already been through the pain of cancer, of losing first her husband's love then actually losing her husband. During the last couple of months she had begun to quietly date an old high school sweetheart. I had met him and even a blind man could see that he doted on her. Finally, she was going to be happy.

I remember hearing someone say that if you don't think God has a sense of humor, make a plan. As I get older, it gets easier to find a place in my life for these little funny but true sayings to fit. Just when she'd found someone to love and to trust, someone who wanted to be a part of her life forever, forever became a question mark.

Soon after that last conversation, Jackie quit calling as frequently. There was a point in time when we talked nearly every day, if only for a few minutes. Now when we talked, she was distant and withdrawn. I knew something was wrong but I had to let her have her privacy. Cancer is a highly personal thing and I did not want to pry. I wanted her to confide in me when she was ready and on her own terms.

On the occasions when we talked, her conversations were short and to the point. She'd ask how I was doing and before I could tell her or ask about her, she'd act like she had another call waiting. "I'm just calling to check on you and I'll talk to you later," she would say. I was beginning to lose my patience, I wanted my friend back, and she acted like she had no time for me.

At some point, I ran into a mutual friend at the mall and as we were catching up on things, she mentioned how sorry she was about Jackie's condition. "What about Jackie's condition?" I asked, not wanting to have this conversation with this woman.

What she told me was that Jackie was being told by her doctors that her cancer was not responding to treatment. In fact, the cancer was spreading. Then as if she had let out a national secret, she assured me that Jackie's mother had told her mother and that's how she knew.

I drove directly to Jackie's house and even this time she tried to focus the conversation on something else. "Jackie Preston," I used the name I always used to let her know I was dead serious. "I've had enough of this not talking to me. Just so you know, I know what's going on. Baby, when were you going to tell me?"

"I'm just processing it right now," she looked at me then looked away. "Just let me process it right now."

Those were the same words she had used the first time around. What the heck did that really mean in the scheme of things?

I wanted to respect her wishes and let her have some privacy. "Jackie, God will do it," I promised.

I was attending church regularly and on Sunday
I shared Jackie's story with my pastor and asked the
congregation for prayer. My pastor had a Word for Jackie and I
was to remind her that all things are possible with God.

Later that day, I went over to spend some time with
Jackie and to share with her the good news from my church.
We managed to laugh at something funny, I don't remember
what, and she seemed so tired. I didn't want to keep her long. I
just wanted to spend a little time with her.

We hugged and kissed goodbye as we always did and
she confided in me that she was going to go away for a couple
of days. She told me that she loved me and she wanted me to
know it. I responded with the same answer. With us it was not a
cliché, we meant it from the bottom of our hearts.

After a couple of days of not hearing from Jackie,
I decided to call to see how her trip had gone. Mrs. Green,
Jackie's mom, answered the phone and when I asked to speak
to Jackie she simply said Jackie was no longer with us. Not
getting the gist of her conversation I responded by asking if she
was still out of town.

I felt what she said before she uttered another word.
"No sweetheart, Jackie died yesterday. I would have called you
but I just couldn't. Not just yet." The sadness in her voice cut
to the quick. Mothers are not built to outlive their children. It
should be the other way around.

Jackie, Mrs. Green told me, was driving and had exited the expressway when she died. The car had come to a stop with one wheel on the curb and the other on the street. Other drivers noticed that there was a woman behind the wheel and believed the car was still running. They notified the police. When the police arrived, Jackie was dead.

"Don't say another word, I'm on my way."

I drove like the wind to a friend who would never be there again. I talked to God, asking Him to receive her into heaven. I asked my own mother to look out for her when she got there and to show her the ropes.

And then the screams came. I screamed for Jackie, and my mom, and John, and for everything and everybody that I'd lost. I paid no attention to people looking at me. I paid no attention to the speed limit. And then I screamed for Jackie's children and her newfound companion, and I screamed for me. I screamed for old and new. I had lost my best friend just one short year after John had been sent to prison.

That night, I was no longer able to push away the need for a drink. On my way home, I stopped at the liquor store and bought a fifth of cognac. I sat in my driveway measuring my pain by the burn of the alcohol. I pushed the half filled bottle beneath the driver's seat because I was already ashamed of my weakness.

CHAPTER 22

Hundreds of people attended Jackie's funeral to celebrate her life. Just as she had reached out to me in the beginning, she had done the same for a couple of hundred people and they all came to say goodbye.

It isn't often that ex-husbands get the opportunity to have a word but Jackie's ex told the congregation that she was a remarkable woman, that she was filled with love and giving, that she was a good wife and an excellent mother. He was able to show more compassion for her in death than he could muster in life and in that single moment in time, I was able to forgive him for the way he had treated her. I may not have walked in his shoes, but I knew a thing or two about loving and losing. Like Jackie, I now pray for him and for the children even when I am incapable of praying for myself.

Someone familiar with Jackie and me and what we meant to each other sent me a poem after Jackie's death. I've hung on to this poem for years because it defines Jackie. She was at first my gift, then my friend, later my sister, my sister-girl, my mother, my reason to hope, my teacher. She stood in my corner without judgment, she felt it her duty to make me laugh even in the midst of pain. She stood in the gap. She prayed for me when I could not pray for myself. She simply was!

People come into your life for a reason, a season or a lifetime.
When you figure out which one it is,
you will know what to do for each person.

When someone is in your life for a REASON,
it is usually to meet a need you have expressed.
They have come to assist you through a difficulty;
to provide you with guidance and support;
to aid you physically, emotionally or spiritually.
They may seem like a godsend, and they are.
They are there for the reason you need them to be.

Then, without any wrongdoing on your part or at an
inconvenient time,
this person will say or do something to bring the relationship to
an end.
Sometimes they die. Sometimes they walk away.
Sometimes they act up and force you to take a stand.
What we must realize is that our need has been met, our desire
fulfilled; their work is done.
The prayer you sent up has been answered and now it is time to
move on.

Some people come into your life for a SEASON,
because your turn has come to share, grow or learn.
They bring you an experience of peace or make you laugh.
They may teach you something you have never done.
They usually give you an unbelievable amount of joy.
Believe it. It is real. But only for a season.

LIFETIME relationships teach you lifetime lessons;
things you must build upon in order to have a solid emotional
foundation.
Your job is to accept the lesson, love the person,
and put what you have learned to use in all other relationships
and areas of your life.
It is said that love is blind but friendship is clairvoyant.

— *Unknown*

Returning to my church after we lost Jackie was bitter sweet. Once again I felt God had taken someone from me that I needed to complete my life. I had always thought Jackie and I would be together for a lifetime and now she was gone. I don't think you get many "best girlfriends" in one lifetime, and except for Ma Wiley, Zita and the children, I was beginning to feel pretty alone.

Pastor Bridget called me to the front of the church and told the congregation that I had just lost my best friend. She asked for prayer for me and my family and prayer for Jackie's family. Voices began to ring out as they lifted Jackie up to God. They prayed the prayer of a million tongues for Jackie's children and mom and all of her loved ones. They prayed for me to be strong in God and for me to be still and know that He was God.

CHAPTER 23

We were now deep into the second year after the investigation began and my personal strip poker game with life continued at a fevered pitch and I continued to lose. Ma Wiley and the children and I bonded tighter and they held on to me helping to keep me just this side of sanity.

Ma Wiley and I talked about Jackie for long stretches of time and in that way she helped me to sum up her life and death. She thought if I could talk about what made Jackie so important to my life, then I could keep the good close to me to gather strength from. Besides the obvious things, like her saving me from myself time and time again, or sitting in court with me, or vacationing with us, where was the substance of our relationship. Today I can honestly say that in death, Jackie made me have an appreciation for motherhood.

As a child, I always wanted to have a house full of children of my own. Before my brother came along, I always prayed for a baby sister. My parents repeatedly told the story of my praying for a sister before meals. As a couple, they took a lot of ribbing for that prayer. Finally, when I was six, my prayers were answered, even if the baby wasn't a girl.

Boys are different and by the time he turned six, I was twelve. He was a nuisance and I was on my way to being a teenager. During those years, we were distanced by gender and time. He was into frogs and kick ball. He wanted to watch action figures on television and play with his little nasty friends who hated water and always smelled like it. I had girl things and was somewhat anxious to wear lipstick and flip my hair. My friends and I giggled a lot and hated certain little boys but liked a handful of slightly older cute ones.

The bond was strained between my brother and me and as the years went on we became distanced by school and later university. Later still, we were able to bridge the age and gender gap and he became my brother, my friend and my champion. I secretly consoled myself with the fact that when I was grown and married, I'd have sixteen children. Just the right amount of boys and girls so that nobody would be lonely in my house. Thankfully, some prayers are not meant to be answered.

No matter still, John and I had been blessed with four children, three boys and a girl. The perfect number. While I naturally brought certain things into my life from my own parents, those things were as a memory of what I felt as a child. Being Jackie's friend gave me an adult close-up view on motherhood and the loving of the lives that have been entrusted to you.

Sometimes I wondered if Jackie knew she wasn't going to be around to see her children grow up and so she wanted them to remember that she was the best. But then I came to the conclusion that she was the best because of who they were and not because of what was happening to her.

Jackie invested more time in her children than anybody I know. Shortly after they were born, she didn't want to put them in day care. They needed time to bond with their mother and she took off a little longer than the usual six weeks. She took responsibility for everything. She expressed milk on a schedule so that they would be nurtured by the best milk possible. When she learned she had cancer the first time, she immediately changed to what she believed to be a more healthy diet. She made a point of changing her children's diet as well and they stuck with it as a family. She never wanted her illness to befall them.

I think she had a plan for each of them before they left her womb. She chose carefully the schools they would attend and the people with whom they could spend time. She guarded their influences not allowing the outside world to get a hold of their young minds. She hugged and kissed them throughout the day and even when she chastised them, she ended it by telling them how much she loved them.

There wasn't a cookie she couldn't bake or a sore that she could not heal on tiny legs and arms. She was the best story teller in the world and constantly made up stories with her children as the center of the tale. Her house was a reflection of the love she had for them and to watch them together when I visited was a blessing.

To put it simple, they adored her.

Jackie was the first in our circle to give her child a theme birthday party. When eventually we caught up with her in the birthday party giving, we paled in comparison. She made magic with her own two hands and created decorations that we couldn't even hope to buy.

After the divorce, even thought I know it hurt her dearly, she insisted that her husband be with them as often as possible. She insisted he come to their house and that he take them to visit at his house. She was determined that her children would have two wonderful parents even if they were divorced. She wasn't selfish when it came to them and what was best for their lives.

Through all of this, she still managed to be a blessing to me and so many others. I can only hope to be half the mother that she was.

CHAPTER 24

In June, near the end of the second year after John was sent to federal prison, I decided to take the children on vacation. We had made a practice of taking them to new places to vacation and I wanted this trip to be special for them. After all, it was the first vacation we'd had as a family unit in such a very long time. I chose the Turks and Caicos Island, a beautiful vacation spot just southeast of Mayaguana in the Bahamas. Sun, sea, fun; the perfect getaway.

This was to be our first vacation since Tahiti, a place I can't bear to think of without bittersweet pain. As much as I enjoyed it, I don't think I will ever be able to go back there again. After the trial, I lost the house as well and found that life goes on. Jackie's untimely death was too painful for words, and I found that no matter what happens, life goes on.

The children had been through as much or more than I had. They had lost both parents for longer than I was willing to admit. They had to come to terms with their father being in prison and their mother being emotionally unavailable for a while afterwards. Then there was Jackie. She was the aunt that they had never had and her loss was felt throughout my family. But it was vacation time and I helped them to get in the spirit of things by promising them that we'd have more fun than they could possibly imagine.

I let them participate by getting brochures about things to do on the island. Naturally the boys chose to see JoJo the

Dolphin. They were excited by anything of the sea, and since they could not see the migrating whales, JoJo was the next best thing. My baby girl, on the other hand, wanted to island hop. She just wanted to see everything she could fit in while we were there. If it was doable by children of their ages, then it became a part of the plan.

And then there was me. I needed to do something mindless for a while. If I was somewhere where I was not known, then maybe I could let my hair down and have some fun. It had been so long since I had done anything just for me. Maybe after the children were down for the evening, one night I could get a sitter and slip away for a while. This could be the relief I sought so that we could move forward as a family.

When I made our reservations, I planned ahead to fly out of Dallas which would give us a chance to visit John who was being held in a federal prison in Texarkana. Even though he was incarcerated, he still needed to be a big part of our lives. The children enjoyed their time with him tremendously and the next day we boarded a plane and headed to the islands.

Once we got settled into the flight and the usual jockeying for position had quieted down, I thought I'd read a bit, then drift off to sleep. Being the intuitive type with my children, I thought something may be wrong as my son, Jason, wasn't getting into mischief. I always had to say stop, quit, and don't when we were on a plane. Stop kicking the back of the seat. Quit bothering your sister or brother. Don't do that anymore. It was a never ending battle to get him to settle down, but not on this flight.

Something's up, I thought. Maybe he's missing his father already. When questioned, he responded that he had a headache. I chalked it up to the visit with his dad and the excitement of the trip, and the fact that we all needed rest. By the time we landed he seemed fine and I basically forgot about the headache.

On the third day of our vacation, Jason seemed very tired. Normally a rambunctious child, constantly moving and running and getting into things, he opted instead to sit in the hot tub and loll around. He was no longer excited about seeing JoJo the Dolphin or anything else we came up with. Frankly, I thought he may be coming down with the flu or a virus and I gave him a Tylenol.

We continued to have a bunch of fun and were all good and tired for the flight back to Houston. As soon as we were strapped into our seats, we all fell asleep. A while later, I woke up and checked the children as I normally do at home. My baby girl was in a stage of her life where she tried to do everything I did, so she was awake and reading. The boys were still asleep and I notice Jason had beads of sweat on his forehead. Later still, the other two boys slowly came awake, yet Jason slept nearly all the way back home, rousing only when we touched down.

The following day, I dropped the children off at Ma Wiley's house and warned her that I thought Jason may have a virus. The other children exhibited no signs of illness. Later in the morning, Ma Wiley called to inform me that Jason had a red rash over most of his body. We discussed her bringing him down to me. When I got a good look at him, I hopped into the car and drove directly to the hospital emergency room.

As a rule, it's usually better to seek treatment from your personal physician, but I needed to know if my son was contagious. My first thought was that I did not want him to contaminate anybody else with the bug which he'd caught. Following the evaluation and within thirty minutes of drawing several vials of blood for test, an Emergency Room Physician reported to me that Jason's blood showed some abnormalities and they thought it best that a Hematologist view the results. I waited and watched over my child as he slept as though he had not slept for days. When at last the physician returned, he asked to see me privately.

My heart skipped a beat. Blood pounded in my ears. Fear gripped my bowel turning it to liquid. I did not want to take another step with these people. What I wanted was to go back to that bay and pick up my baby and take him home and cure him of whatever it was. But I couldn't. I had to listen to what the physician had to say.

With a counselor present, I learned my child was indeed very sick. His blood count was critically low. They came to the point quickly. Jason had Leukemia.

The fragile peace of mind that I had managed to tag together over the past few months fractured and shattered into a zillion tiny pieces as I yelled at the top of my lungs. "Not my baby! Lord, please, not my baby!" I yelled as though it mattered to anybody but me. "I've lost almost everybody who was close to me to Cancer. I've lost my mother at a time when I needed her most." I rambled on. People down the hall got an ear full of what I had been through. "I just lost my best friend. Who am I kidding, she was my only friend, to a fight that she could not win. Can't you see, I can't lose my baby! I would lose my mind." I spun around searching for something, anything. I came to rest with my arms over my head, drained and pleading for something they could not give. "I'm already hanging on by a thread. So please just take it back this one time. Give me back my baby. Please listen to me. This is not meant for Jason, he hasn't done anything wrong." But they couldn't turn time back. They could only move forward.

CHAPTER 25

Where to go and what to do? I forced myself to calm down so that I would be able to help my child. I could finish my breakdown later, but right now, I was all this child had for a parent in that hospital and I knew I need lots of information in order to snatch him from the jaws of cancer.

Information came overwhelmingly from every corner. The hospital was prepared for cases like ours and they shifted into gear. Starting immediately, Jason had to be admitted to the hospital where he'd stay for at least a month and where he'd start chemotherapy immediately. Because the chemotherapy would further weaken his immune system, he'd fare better if he was not allowed to be around other people. For him, school became a thing of the past. Doctors figured he'd be isolated at home for at least a year as we battled the cancer.

They talked incessantly and half of my brain listened scholarly, while the other half contained my break down. When I could take no more, I simply shut down. I was physically incapable of dealing with anybody or anything.

Stumbling from the room, I made my way outside where I gulped air like a drowning man. This is why I need my husband, I thought. He was somewhere laid back on a prison cot, doing whatever it is that people do in prison and I had to deal with this kind of thing a-l-o-n-e.

What to do now? Where was Jackie? God, how I needed Jackie to tell me that everything was going to be just fine, that this too would pass. But Jackie was not there. John was not there. My mother was not there. Everybody had managed somehow to leave me and every time I thought I was on the mend, something else happened to knock me back down.

Where was God? What had I done to deserve to be left out of the protection of God? Tears cascaded from my eyes and I could barely see. I began to beseech God for mercy. If not for me, surely for my six-year-old child who had done nothing to deserve this pain. He deserved a child's life. He deserved a mother and a father. He deserved to go home and to play with his sister and brothers. He deserved better than what John and I had given him. He deserved life. What he got instead was a father behind bars, a mother that was functioning at less than half of her normal self, a piecemeal family, a sick bed with doctors poking holes into his skinny arms, and dangerous chemicals entering his weakened system.

CHAPTER 26

I needed answers. And, I needed a drink.

I was going to have to take more bad news to my other children and Ma Wiley. But I had to get myself together before I could do that.

My stomach was beginning to feel the effects of not having eaten for most of the day and I stopped at a restaurant where I knew the food was decent. Seated alone, I ordered something to eat and the waiter asked if I'd like something to drink while I waited for them to prepare my food.

I ordered a Martini, very dry. And then a second. I still needed answers but at the moment, there was no urgency. The alcohol made me feel a little lightheaded and afterwards, the food tasted better than I remembered.

After finishing my meal, and on the way out of the door, I abruptly turned around and went to the restaurant bar. Seated amid people that seemed not to have a care in the world, I ordered a Manhattan. I pretended to be with the group nearest me. Overhearing some of their conversation, when they laughed, I laughed. As the conversation moved freely I pretended to answer questions and moved my lips as I toasted the entire bar.

Downing my third drink at the bar, I opened my mouth to ask for a fourth and the bartender shook his head. He was through serving me. Since I wasn't drunk, I thought I'd go to the restroom and then drive myself home. Holding on to the wall, I managed to make my way to the door marked "Ladies" just as the alcohol collided with the portabella mushroom burger and fries that I'd eaten earlier.

The tiny restroom began to spin and swirl around dragging me with it to the floor. Sweat was running down my neck and I was hot beyond belief. Relieved to find the tile cool when I finally touched the floor, I turned my face from side to side so that my cheeks would cool as well. My stomach lurched a couple of times as I crawled to the toilet on my hands and knees. Between short trips to the floor and the toilet, I got the understanding that I was drunk.

People came and went and I recall somebody asking if I needed help. I suppose I was convincing when I said that I was fine or something to the effect. After a while I was able to wash my face and walk out of the restaurant, finally sober enough to drive myself home.

Things always look better in the light of day. The following morning, I broke the news of Jason's illness to my family. I hugged the three of them with Ma Wiley looking on as I promised them that their brother would get well and be home soon. Then, I called my dad in Canada for the first time in a long time, and told him how much I needed him. By the end of the week, he was in Houston and ready to help us wherever he could.

I knew I couldn't handle this by myself anymore and I called my church family and asked for prayer and intercession on behalf of my child. They set up a prayer circle and prayed ceaselessly for my child and for me and my family. They mentioned fasting and praying until something broke in the supernatural. I knew that they believed and that would have to hold me until I could do better for myself.

I also knew that I could not take another drink of alcohol. The comfort that was stashed beneath my car seat would have to go. Today!

CHAPTER 27

The hospital was a top-notch institution and they wanted to involve me in every stage of Jason's treatment. They wanted to give me a tour of the facility and to walk me through the treatment. I could not participate in this.

My mind was not ready to fully embrace what was happening to my child. I specifically told them that they were allowed to do whatever was necessary for my child but that I absolutely could not be brought along for the viewing. I later realized what I had done was detached myself as a survival mechanism. If I could close it off, if I could shut it out of my mind, it would not exist.

One day while I was seated by Jason's bedside, looking at his angelic face as he slept, the thought came to me that I did not want cancer mentioned to him in any way. This feeling was so strong that I went directly to the nurse's station and made the request asking that it be put in his chart. I went further and asked his doctors to not mention the word cancer in front of him. At the lab, I made specific request that the word cancer not be mentioned in front of my child. I became adamant about not mentioning cancer to my son or in conjunction with his treatment or with his name and I began to decorate his room with Scriptures. The hospital staff and his physicians honored my request.

As is customary for most chemotherapy recipients, the side effects were devastating for Jason. He was plagued with nausea and vomiting, and a fever, and he lost his hair. He absolutely would not eat. Whenever a doctor or a nurse would enter his room he would hide his little face under the covers calling out for me or his father. He had so many blood tests that in time, he knew exactly why they were there. He was pumped with so much medicine and steroids that his physical features changed drastically. His body was puffy and I could no longer see the beautiful boy that I knew him to be. He became withdrawn when he wasn't feeling good and he slept constantly. All I knew was that no matter how he looked, or how sick he was, he was mine and I loved him with every breath in my body. While Jason was helpless, I was determined not to be.

As a pharmacist, I am considered a medical professional. I understand cancer, I understand what it does to the body, I understand treatment, I understand cure and no cure, and I understand what a patient goes through. My mother and my best friend both died from cancer and as much as I hated that fact, they were both grown. They had both tasted life.

Not so with Jason. Six short years was all he'd had. If I let myself think about it, he may never run like a deer again, he may never walk across a stage to get a diploma, he may never have his first crush, and he may never know the joys of marriage and fatherhood. Jason had not yet begun to live and six years old was so very young. I was incapable of understanding why this had to happen to my baby.

When John and I were selecting a name for Jason, I immediately wanted to name him Jericho Wiley. That name just seemed to fit my spirit. John wouldn't hear of it. He didn't want his son to be ridiculed at school. Children can be so cruel, and he didn't want his son hurt by complete strangers. I acquiesced and we named him Jason Jericho Wiley. Days that I sat in his room watching his body fight to overcome infection after infection, I began to think that I may have been prophetic in wanting to name him Jericho. Walls literally had to come down for him.

CHAPTER 28

Things the doctors told me to expect manifested in my baby's body. After his first release from the hospital, we were in and out of there constantly. The least little sneeze, or cough, ear infection, a sore throat, a sore that would not heal, and he would be admitted. Some type of infection or exposure would cause his blood counts to plummet to a critical level and he'd need a blood transfusion, or plasma. I felt the pain of his illness almost as much as he did. Suffering and six years old should not have to be mentioned in the same sentence.

In between all of this, I learned that if Jason weathered this storm, he could be in treatment for up to three years or better. He would have to miss a whole year from school. He was experiencing loss after loss after loss. His father, his siblings, his teachers, his friends, his pets. It was all being taken from him. Running, playing, football, catch, sharing, arguments, fights with his sister and brothers.

I began to have a new worry. Depression. Not my depression. Jason's depression. I didn't want him to feel sorry for himself. It was only natural but I just didn't want him to suffer that way.

There were times when he'd ask me if he was going to die. No matter what I thought, my words slipped out easily. "Of course not darling, you're getting better every day. I know sometimes it doesn't feel like it, but you are." It was times like these that I'd love on him as I prayed to God to make my words be the truth for him. "Please, God, don't let me lie to him about this."

Even though he was gravely ill, I wanted Jason's life to have some kind of normalcy, I prayed for God to show me the way to help him and help came in the form of two of his teachers. Ms. Jones and Ms. Adams volunteered to come to our home and teach Jason for a year. That was quite a commitment and they were faithful. Although he could not be around children, his friends from football and their parents constantly inquired about him. Little things were always coming in the mail for him. A homemade card, a letter, an action figure, a T-shirt, always some little something.

At the end of the first year, Jason was finally stable enough to return to school. Before his illness, he was a normal six-year-old. Jason on chemotherapy was a different person. Whereas his grades were very good prior to chemo, on chemo, he found it difficult to focus and retain lessons learned and what was an upwardly mobile six-year-old became a "C", "D" and sometimes "F" seven-year-old. Another worry, another hurdle to jump. I talked things over with Dad and Ma Wiley and John and we settled on changing schools in order to get another perspective.

Teachers at the new school did not know Jason's history and they encouraged us to hold him back for another year giving him time to catch up with his classmates. I was about to agree with this theory until Ma Wiley clearly pointed out that Jason might suffer psychologically from being held back. He had already lost too much, to allow him to fail could easily cause irreparable damage. I knew I'd have to find another way.

Without looking for special treatment, I met with Jason's teachers and explained our situation. They were compassionate and made the decision to allow him to advance with his class. That was a prayer answered. Once off of chemotherapy, Jason's capacity to learn and recall details returned and his grades improved drastically.

CHAPTER 29

After Jackie's death, I had become more faithful in my spiritual life. I don't pretend to understand all that my family and I were going through, but I was praying more, coping better, and stumbling less. Make no mistake, Jason's illness, on top of all of the other things, almost broke my spirit.

While Jason was still in the hospital, I was headed for home after a grueling week of taking care of everybody's needs as much as I could. He had been particularly nauseous and up-chucked most of the morning. There wasn't much I could do except wipe his face with a cool towel and pray for this latest round of sickness to ease. Barely driving the speed limit, my mind was flitting from one thing to the next. I thought, God, I was tired and when did I get this old.

I pulled the car over on the expressway and looked at myself, really looked at myself. My hair was dry and limp. . Looking back at me from the mirror was a face that I almost didn't recognize. My eyes were larger than I remembered and wide with something behind them. Was it fear, or was I just waiting for the other foot of fate to drop on me? My lips were dry and chapped. I reached for my bag, retrieved some lipstick and slashed it across my lips. There, I thought, that's better. This time when I smiled, the face that smiled back was slightly better, but a dab of lipstick can't begin to erase a hard life from your neck up. The face that looked back at me had aged considerably.

Easing the car back into traffic, my first thought was to just drive around until I felt better. I found myself passing the exit where Jackie was found in her car. As I came up to the next exit, I quickly got off and made a U-turn to go back down the feeder. Already in a blue funk, I slowed and looked to see if I could see Jackie. My God, I thought, she's not coming back and I struggled to catch my breath. In a hurry now and for no reason at all, I heard my car tires squeal as I accelerated. I needed to get away.

By dusk, I had put some distance between me and Houston, between me and my problems, between me and everybody that needed something from me. Beaumont was behind me and I had no idea where I was headed. Interstate 10 ran for miles ahead of me on into Louisiana and Alabama, and Florida. I had no place to go and no certain time to be there. I was running away because I was running out of time and people to leave me and people to die. God was letting all of this happen and I was just sick and tired. It had all fallen on me to make sense of things and to pull us back together. I could not do it anymore.

I just couldn't take the pressures anymore. I desperately needed to be free if only for one night.

CHAPTER 30

Most of the time it seemed like the laughter had gone out of my soul, a light had been shut off and I was constantly in one state of darkness or the other. Jackie and Ma Wiley were my "rocks." Jackie had been there since college and I loved her like she was my blood sister. If fact, she became the sister I had always wanted.

If I considered my wedding day as one of the happiest days of my life, and it was, then it would be fitting for me to say that was also the day I married a family, John and Ma Wiley.

She had always accepted me, first as John's fiancé and later as his young bride.

I felt kindly toward her because I love John. How could I not like the person who had brought him into the world and raised him to be the kind of person that I wanted to father my children?

I had already heard too many bad mother-in-law jokes and how they wrecked havoc in most marriages. Ma Wiley is a saint when compared to other mother-in-laws I'd heard about.

She is a woman of great strength and compassion. You'd think with only one child, she'd be selfish with him, that she'd used up all of her love on him. She had taken an active part in raising and educating John and took much due pride in his accomplishments. That included him marrying a like-minded woman. Ma Wiley went above and beyond to make me feel a part of her family and I began to love her because of that. Adding grandbabies to the mix cemented our relationship. I never knew anyone could love another human being as much as she loved my children,

A few years after we were married, my own mother became gravely ill with colon cancer and we knew she was not going to recover. Ma Wiley reached out to me and my family with all of the compassion she possessed. My mother knew she was about to leave us and was more worried about my brother and me than she was about her fate. Ma Wiley made a promise to my mother that she would be a mother to me and the best grandmother in the world to my children. She did not take her promise lightly and as my young family began to grow, she was a woman of her word.

When disaster struck and John was arrested and tried for crimes which we all believed he did not commit, Ma Wiley presented herself in court every day for both trials in support of John and me. It was almost a year from the day he was arrested until the day he was finally sentenced. In the scheme of things, not a very long time, but taken individually, it was a year that she put her life on hold and concentrated on John's and my wellbeing. Instead of enjoying the freedom of her years, she found herself pressed into service as a fixer.

John and I had not decided what we were going to tell our children about what we were going through. We knew that we did not want to discuss the exact charges with them nor the possibility of their dad having to go to jail. We wanted to protect them for as long as possible. We limited their exposure to the outside world and were careful not to leave papers around or to let them watch television news whatsoever. Not that they were interested in such things, we just didn't want there to be the slightest chance they would hear anything concerning this case.

Ma Wiley made it possible for us to avoid the entrapments of other people. She became the go-to person for the family. If there was a problem that I could not handle, Ma Wiley was the person who made everything disappear. While I managed to hold myself together during the actual trial hours, I did not do so well with the balance of the day. She became the "soccer mom," picking the children up and dropping them off and seeing that they were fed and told them that they were loved.

Once John was incarcerated, we got busy with the appeals process. Both Ma Wiley and I were in concert about not giving up on his freedom. And, she and Jackie made sure I also did not give up on the house. They thought I should fight for it for the sake of the children. I, on the other hand, was not so certain. I came around to seeing things their way and gave it my all.

The fight for the house pushed me to the brink and Jackie and Ma Wiley snatched me back. I made an attempt to thank them both by presenting Ma Wiley with a healthy and beautiful grandson and by naming the baby in Jackie's honor. The baby whom I had called my symbol of hope was named Jaxon. His name would always be a constant reminder of my feelings for Jackie. Her name would be on my lips every time I called my son's name.

I attempted to make my children my top priority through everything that had happened to us. Sometimes that meant not sharing things with them. I wanted their lives to be as normal as possible. When I could not think straight for myself, I tried to hone in on their lives and make the best decisions for them.

Even though I almost lost my sanity with the loss of the house, I physically had to let it go. Somewhere, I had the temerity to tell my children that we were just tired of working on that old house and we were glad to finally be rid of it. As they grew older, I measured how much of the whole truth they should have privy to. One day they will know it all.

While Jason was still ill but definitely on the mend, I knew I had to make a decision to get back to work. What little money I had saved, independent of John, was running out faster than even I had anticipated. Ma Wiley had given me financial assistance along with moral support. She had been what I needed her to be but I could not continue to take advantage of her generosity. I absolutely had to have an income. She pitched in with my dad to continue taking care of the children while I got back on my feet.

I reasoned that with Jason being sick the older children would be on their own far too often if I took a position with one of the chains. My work hours would more than likely be odd shifts, which for a pharmacy is standard, and could also stand to works nights and weekends. Ma Wiley and my dad had already pitched in more than their fair share and I had to make an effort to give them both some of their life back.

CHAPTER 31

The children were getting of a certain age where I knew now was not the time for them to be without the constant presence of both parents. Since I couldn't be gone most of the time, I had to find the solution that was best for my family. I racked my brain looking for a solution. I wanted to open my own business but I was afraid the government might swoop down and take it from me, claiming that it was financed with monies from John's business.

The pharmacy circle is small enough for news to circulate rapidly and I had heard of a young pharmacist who was looking to go into business. Calling her up, we talked about pooling our efforts. She agreed to take the risk of allowing me to be a silent partner in an attempt to protect me and herself from harassment from the government, should they be inclined to do so. She and I got along well and tried to make a go of our small business. It takes time to build consumer confidence and a lot of hard work to secure the kind of client base we needed to support two households.

My partner needed the business to be profitable almost immediately, which is almost unheard of in any small business. I suspected the difference in our age and the fact that our goals were not the same contributed in part to the decision we came to some six short months later. I needed to rebuild my life, one step at a time. She needed to earn money now.

Looking back, I can see clearly that this business was destined to fail. I had entered into the partnership out of fear. I was afraid that if I opened a store alone, the government would come after me trying to prove I had used funds from John's pharmacy to start this business and I would be back in the same place where I was trying to leave.

We put the business up for sale and split the proceeds. I took my half of the money and opened a pharmacy. My attitude quickly became one of confidence. I had done nothing wrong before and I was doing nothing wrong now. I had long ago come to the conclusion that everybody and everything had to be what it would be. I did not care what the government did, I needed to provide for my children, and as single women do everyday all over this land, I threw caution to the wind, said my prayers and stepped out in faith.

I devoted most of my waking hours to getting the business up and running. I opened the store in the mornings and worked until one in the afternoon. I filled prescriptions, made deliveries, marketed my business and services, served as a janitorial crew of one doing floors and windows without complaint. I was gone from home from very early in the morning until around 6:00 p. m.

Ma Wiley, Zita, and Dad shared the job of taking care of the children. They split the duties of shuttling the children back and forth, babysitting, cooking, taking confessions, dispensing discipline and freely giving daytime kisses and hugs. She picked the kids up each morning and dropped them off at school and he picked them up in the afternoon and stayed with them until I returned home.

Ma Wiley and Dad were thrust into a role that they had not had a hand in for over twenty years. They shared the burden of attending school functions, parent-teacher conferences, tended colds, and scrapes, checked homework, and constantly told the children how much John and I loved them. The three of us banded together to make a family. I had no other life outside of work, church, and home and neither did Ma Wiley or Dad. By the end of that year, the pharmacy was profitable and I was no longer worried about the never ending bills.

I owed Ma Wiley more than I could ever repay and I will be eternally grateful for the role she played in all of our lives. Without us asking, she proved her love for us over and over again in ways that were unimaginable.

My dad and I developed an adult father-daughter relationship. I must say that as a young woman, I never knew the man who showed up at my home to lend me a hand. I had never seen him in the light that he presented. He took over the house and developed a schedule for it to run on. He gave my children stability and the firm hand of a loving and compassionate male. He gave me his shoulder to cry on and removed it when he'd seen and heard enough. He did not enable me and insisted that I take full responsibility for my "now." He encouraged me to not only fly but to soar. In time, I would not only come to the same conclusion but to also embrace it.

CHAPTER 32

At one of the lowest moments in my life and after John was in prison, a young woman appeared from out of nowhere to say that John had bought her a car and she needed money with which to make the payment or they would take the car. The irony of this incident smacked me in the face. I listened as she tried for whatever reasons to get money from me. Perhaps she thought I would just pay for her car, or perhaps she thought that she was entitled to something as she intimated that she was John's mistress.

My life was in such upheaval I could not entertain what she tried to tell me. I felt nothing for her or about her. It is a possibility that she may have had a relationship with my husband, but clearly she had not had one with me or my children and I was not about to add a burden that I was not a party to. As usual, I told Ma Wiley about the young lady and in her infinite wisdom, she made the issue go away. I didn't ask how or what the outcome may have been. I simply did not want to know.

Later when I visited John, I mentioned the incident and he vehemently denied any wrong doing on his part and has maintained that stance to this day. I let the matter go for the moment, but harbored the thought until it festered and became the straw that finally broke the camel's back.

Whereas, I believed John had done nothing wrong to land himself in prison, I did not believe he had not had an affair and the thought was like a double edge sword. I wondered what else he'd lied to me about. How many other women were there? Had he thought he was in love with somebody else? What had I done to make him forget his marriage vows? I had no answers and with each question numbness expanded within me until I felt nothing.

With the pharmacy turning a profit and Jason on the mend, I had a little more time to go around. I should have been feeling good but I wasn't. I was feeling nothing. That's scary. It's worse than thinking nothing. Days went by and the feeling grew deeper. Unlike when I was depressed and cried at the drop of a hat, I felt like I would never cry over anything again, that it would make no difference what happened from here on out. I was on rote and nothing mattered anymore. I was all about doing what I had to do. I didn't like this feeling and thought it was not in my best interest to continue on this path. Many things had changed in my life and I was learning to trust my feelings.

Almost daily for the four and a half years since John was arrested, I had told myself that I could not take anymore. I had told this to John, Jackie and Ma Wiley, Dad and to Pastor Bridget, to my attorneys, to Jason's doctors and anybody else within ear shot.

I now knew that it was all over for me. The suffering was over, the depression was over, the grieving was complete, the total and absolute dependence on a process was done, my marriage was done and I was the only person that knew this.

I owed it to my children to explain my decision to get a divorce once I was certain that was the path I should take. The four of us sat together as I attempted to share with them that I would be getting a divorce. I had to explain to the smaller ones what a divorce was. I made it clear that I was not asking for permission to get a divorce. The decision was an adult decision and they did not get to participate like they did when we chose cold cereal.

My oldest son already had friends with divorced parents and he wasn't happy about John and me doing the same thing. He burst into tears and begged me for at least two days to reconsider. I heard his pain and I could see it, but I could not feel it. He chose that moment to quit speaking to me. He was not disrespectful, but he said as little to me as was possible. I tried to understand and I uttered such prayers as I could for God to help him through yet another painful period. I had begun to pray for time to heal my children's bodies and spirits. I did this because without Divine intervention, their young lives may be scarred by the sins of their parents.

After the children, I discussed it with my dad. Although he was devout in his faith and did not believe in divorce, he had the presence of mind to allow me to make my own decisions. He had witnessed firsthand my struggle and stood beside me as I began to rebuild my life. He promised to stand with me no matter what decision I made concerning my marriage.

Next, I spoke to Pastor Bridget about my decision. The sanctity of marriage is one of the major tenets of her religious faith and she was none too pleased with my decision. She spoke to me about what God would have me do and I listened to her but I did not change my mind.

What she said did not faze me. I believed God would do what He was going to do no matter what I did. God was in control of our relationship and He did whatever He would do no matter how I begged and pleaded, or cried out to Him or how much I prayed. I needed to make this move for me and me alone.

Then came the day I made the trip to prison to talk with John about getting a divorce. While going through the changes necessary to actually see a prisoner, I remembered the day John asked me to be his bride. I lived the wedding and all of its glory in the short time it took me to get to see my husband. Nothing was rehearsed, when the time was right I simply told him I was tired and that I was going to get a divorce. The weariness of it all was written all over my face. I promised that I would not come between him and the children; that I would support and encourage the idea of two parents just in separate places. I promised that I would help him get back on his feet when he was released from prison. This I did because he was my husband, the father of my children, my first and only love, and even now I still loved him. I would never want to see him harmed. I had simply had all I could take.

John had plenty of time to think while behind bars. He told me he had already resigned himself to the fact that the day would come sooner or later. He just had not expected it for that day. He was not angry. His only wish was that I split whatever

I had left from the funds which were not attached by the courts. Already there was none left and I had to tell him so. The cost of living and using our savings everyday without replenishing them reduced the value quickly. He looked at me as though I was lying, but I did not care. The money was gone.

I had to work every day to make ends meet and I was not in a mood to feel guilty because it was all spent on my children and lawyer fees. I walked away from John without guilt.

From the moment I first scribbled my name with his on a note pad to the moment the prison doors closed behind me, he had been my mate. I had given him all that I had. What I could not give to him any longer was more. I was all used up.

Ma Wiley was the last person that I had told. I know I owed her better but I was fresh out of paying debts. John was her only child and I didn't want it to appear to her that I was walking out on him. I was not walking out. I just had to give in so I could be alive again. I needed to make peace with life.

The divorce was not about Ma Wiley, it was about me. I so appreciated all that she had done for me before and after John went to prison. I was not trying to walk away from her. I wanted to honor our relationship for the rest of my life. But, the time had come. I was emotionally spent and I had nothing else to offer John or anybody else. Ma Wiley was disappointed and I knew it, but she remained steadfast in my life and those of my children.

CHAPTER 33

My life was in turmoil and I kept moving from one tragedy to another, unable to understand what was happening to me. No matter what happened, I continued to seek to be in the presence of God. The church had been a way of life for me since I was a child.

You hear tales about ministers failing to reach out to people in their congregation, and I was no exception. I had heard the elders talk about how some ministers and church people only wanted the saved to attend. They believed that sinners had no place in their congregation. That is, recent sinners. If your sins were old enough to be forgiven by the congregation, then you were welcome.

John and I had joined the largest congregations in Houston and while we were not in the church every time the doors opened, we were there constantly. We paid our tithes and offerings, and considered ourselves a part of the church family. When trouble knocked on our door the first time, we naturally tried to make an appointment for counsel with the pastor. We understood that we'd have to make an appointment with the people responsible for taking care of his calendar, describing the nature of our business. The word was passed back through to us that he would not see us about this matter.

Slapped down before we could begin to rise, I sought to join a church where the pastor and the congregation were a little more sinner friendly. A place where, like the law of the land, they were willing to wait until the verdict was in before they passed judgment. I moved from one church to the next trying to find a place where I was comfortable. I made no attempt to try to get counsel from a stranger minister during that time.

Thankfully, my physician's husband was also a pastor and John and I had worshiped with them several times. These people knew me and knew my history as well, and were comfortable with me. They became my spiritual advisors and waged prayer for us constantly. They organized prayer warriors to send up prayers for our deliverance. .

After the second trial, ashamed and downtrodden, I could not bring myself to face the public and turned to the television to receive my "church". This is where I was first introduced to the preaching of Pastor Bridget. I was mesmerized with her teachings and took the invitation that she extended to the audience to attend a conference where she would be speaking.

Ignited, my friend and I decided to attend the conference. When I count my blessings, I see this chance viewing as one of the most profound things that ever happened to me. I felt that God was reaching out to me, trying to tell me something that maybe I had heard before but had not fully considered for my life.

It is through this ministry that I've learned about deliverance, and forgiveness. I've come to an understanding and full appreciation of the power God has invested in us through his Son Jesus Christ.

Not only is Pastor Bridget anointed, she has also been a friend and a mother to me. After Jackie died, we grew closer as women and she took on the job of mothering me. If I had a problem, I could discuss it with her. From the first day I met her, my spirit was at home and I made it my business to become a responsible member of the church family.

With Jackie gone, and before Jason was diagnosed with cancer, I began to take a more active role in the church and in the choir in particular. Pastor John, Pastor Bridget's husband, wanted to start a choir and he invited the entire church to audition. I had more nerve than talent and went for an audition. Although I had never sang in a church choir, I had been at many a choir practice with my mother and father. She sang soprano and he tenor as I watched and now I hoped that this was enough of an experience to get me in the choir. Jackie would have laughed me under the table for thinking that, but I didn't care, I was going to give it all I had.

Surprisingly, I made the cut. I was nothing spectacular but I was one among the group that sang praise and glory to God. In January of the following year, Pastor Bridget prayed that our spiritual gifts would come to pass. This is where Jackie would have made a joke about us sounding so bad the pastor had to pray for us to get better. She would have probably been accurate in that assessment. Nonetheless, prayer went up to the heavens and slowly we began to sound better.

By March, I was singing and enjoying the feeling. I was frequently told my voice was a blessing and people enjoyed the presence of God when our choir sang. I was glad to be a part of something that was so pleasing to God.

The more I sang the stronger I felt spiritually, and the stronger I felt the more I felt the anointing of God. I grew bolder in Christ and asked to lead the choir at times. I'd stand looking out over the congregation, so nervous my knees were knocking. As I began to sing, I tried to focus on the words of the song and what they meant in my life. It was times such as these that I became strong and was able to sing with a purpose. I glorified His name while singing of His love and grace and a sincere appreciation for God began to flow through me. For the first time in a long time, I felt lifted.

Life's circumstances continued to cause me distress and while I enjoyed singing in the choir, I found it difficult to believe, and without belief, my heart was not in the singing. Each week it became increasingly more difficult for me to sing the songs that spoke about the goodness of God and to praise Him when I thought none of that goodness stretched to cover me and my family.

I have since learned that when we are at our lowest it's also the time that God can use us to spread His Word. I remember a story where there were many people living in an old house, many more than the law deemed acceptable, when one night there came a great fire and fourteen of the fifteen people inside perished. Days later, at the funeral of the fourteen deceased people, there was much dancing and praise and testifying to the goodness of God that things had turned out as good as it was.

They seem to automatically know that everybody in the house would have perished if not for the grace of God.

Life was so hard for me during that five-year journey that I couldn't keep a balance in my faith. Or, was life so hard because I did not keep a balance in my faith? Perhaps I will never know which statement is true but what I know for certain is that I never gave up, I only gave out.

Each time I lost hope, I struggled to find God again, even if I believed he was not answering my prayers. It was the only way I knew to live my life. I'd make great strides and then something else would happen to challenge my thinking and I'd then doubt God. And each and every time I fell down, He was there to lift me up. It took a long time but I learned that there is never an excuse for straying from the protection of God and living an acceptable life before Him.

Pastor Bridget has the gift from God that lets her see thing clearly as they are happening. She knows the nature of man. Whenever I would stray from God, she would reach out to me with words of comfort and try to discuss the things that she knew me to be doing. Like a mother, she'd confront me about my choices and I knew she was disappointed in my behavior. And just like a mother, she never turned her back on me because of the choices I made. She kept praying for me and my family. She was right there each and every time I was challenged by lack of faith to welcome me again into the house of the Lord. She is a woman capable of great love for God and for all of His children and she showed me the palm of her hand every time.

Once, I lashed out to her about something I was doing that she did not care for. Before it happened, I would have sworn I was not capable of such behavior, yet the proof is there. Without thinking, I raised my voice at her telling her to leave me alone and to stay out of my life. That no matter what I did, it was my life to do with as I pleased.

Even as I heard it coming from my mouth, I could not believe I'd said that. She had never done anything to deserve to be talked to in that manner and with that tone of voice. I know if she had said something I did not like, I should have walked away when the moment presented itself.

My words caused pain to spread across her face as though she'd been slapped. This occurred during the same time frame that I decided to get the divorce. I felt nothing. I believed I was incapable of feeling anything else, this time I was giving up.

She suffered, my children suffered, Ma Wiley suffered and John suffered. This was the first time that I did not suffer. I may never cry again. The thought shook me to the core, but my spirit no longer felt a thing.

There were times that no matter how hard I prayed, most of the time I felt God was not listening. In my do-right mind, I knew that was not the case, so when I could, I'd go back to church and try to improve in my prayer life. Back and forth I went and when I was absent, Pastor Bridget would call to check up on me. It got to the point where I monitored my phone calls because I didn't want to hear what she had to say, and still she left little voice mail prayers for me. She let me know that she was still praying for me. She was an expert at standing in the gap.

CHAPTER 34

Pastor Bridget introduced me to many things about God, the church and fulfilling prophecy. In mid-summer of the fifth year since John was sent to prison, she and I had made plans to go to the Global Leadership Conference to participate in a conference hosted by Dr. Miles Munroe of Bahamas Faith Ministries International (BFMI) in Nassau. The focus of this organization is the uplifting of Third World developing nations and people everywhere who are products of oppression. It is a global organization that serves to restore a sense of divine identity, heritage, purpose, potential and destiny to every individual. BFMI is committed to establishing a leadership organization dedicated to setting a precedent, raising a standard, and producing a model of excellence in personal, community and national leadership based on Kingdom values.

It was during this four-day event, where I was part of a body of people from all over the world, that I also had the opportunity to meet Dr. Philip Phinn, a conference participant. Dr. Phinn is the Chief Ambassador to NGO (Non-Government Organizations) and is currently in a consultative status with the United Nations. I had the opportunity to hear him lecture and mistook his accent to be from my island, Trinidad. Feeling a kinship as people are want to do when they are away from their homeland for a long period of time, I thought I'd say hello to him and thank him for his teachings. I had never met the pastor previously and was surprised to learn that he was from Jamaica.

I sat and chatted with him anyway and he shared with me that he was a prophet.

This stranger wanted to know what my missions were in life. He simply asked and I shared with him that I had been through a very trying past few years but that I wanted to do something for people. I felt that I had sat out of life for so long. I now knew I had strength and I was ready to be about the Kingdom's business. On the spot, I told him about the pharmacy and about Jason's cancer and about the desire to eradicate illness for children everywhere. It was a thought and at that moment, I had instant faith that I could make this my life's mission.

I felt something in my spirit yearn for prayer, so I asked him to pray for me. He began a quiet prayer in the natural and mingled it with speaking in tongue. I sat quietly letting his prayer wash over me and draw me nearer. Without hesitancy, he began to prophesy. Then and there, he set out a fifty-six day plan of blessings. During prophecy, he urged me to look out for sudden miracles beginning on the seventh day from that moment forward. He spoke miracles into my life for day twenty-one, and day forty, and on day fifty- six. His prayer was simple. He did not raise his voice, he did not shout, he did not strain, he simply spoke miracles into my life.

On the following day, I ran into Dr. Phinn quite by accident and again we broached the subject of what I saw as a vision for my life. Before I entered college, I knew that I wanted to be in the medical profession. That dream was later refined and my contribution to the profession was by way of dispensing healing medicines. What a blessing it would be if I could also focus some of that calling on a part of the world that desperately needed quality medicine for its people. Thousands of people die each year because of lack of access to healing medications, or from being dispensed substandard pharmaceuticals.

Many things we view in the United States as our rights as citizens are unique unto us. This is not the case for most of the world citizens. There is a constant and oftentimes lost battle for the right pharmaceuticals at the right time to the right patient. I had never wavered from my dream since the beginning, but I was now at a point in my life where I could consider expanding the dream to a full blown mission.

Dr. Phinn and I spoke again shortly after I returned home. We continued to talk about my mission and how I would go about handling God's work as I moved forward in my life. Finally, Dr. Phinn asked if I'd consider being a Non-Governmental Organization Ambassador. Of course my answer was to the affirmative, but I did not know much about the process. He advised me on how to go about filling out the paperwork and urged me to submit my application immediately as the time to submit would soon expire.

Since going into business independently, I had done all of the marketing of services for the pharmacy. A small pharmacy most likely can't survive on walk-in business alone. Things are made easier when you provide a service on a continuous basis to organizations with a specific need like care facilities of all types.

In early December, a friend told me of a facility that was looking for a pharmacy. I placed a call to the facility almost immediately and, to my disappointment, was told they would not do business with me. Life goes on even when the answer is no, so I continued with my day. Nearly six hours later, I received a call from the director of the facility with the news that maybe we could work out a reasonable contract for services.

The following day, day-seven after meeting Dr. Phinn, I signed a lucrative contract with that organization. It was a miracle, something that occurred to improve my lot or station in life that I had not fully expected. I called Dr. Phinn to tell him that the miracles he had spoken into my life were being manifested.

On the first day of December, the twenty-first day after meeting Dr. Phinn, I learned that my application was being submitted for review to the United Nations to become an Ambassador for the Word of Life Ministries International and International Third World Leaders Association. When we submitted my application, it was near the last day that it could be officially submitted for consideration. Several hundred people submit applications each year and many are denied the privilege of serving. I considered this act my second miracle that was manifested from the prophecy of Dr. Phinn.

Later in December, I traveled to Freetown, the capital of Sierra Leone a war torn country in the western sector of Africa. During an eleven-year civil war, thousands of Sierra Leone citizens were uprooted and many of its children were left in a state of poverty and ill health, suffering from a myriad of diseases.

I was accompanied on this trip by four additional Americans and one Sierra Leone native. For five days, we toured the country, taking in the condition of its people and while so doing, I got a feel for what I could hope to accomplish.

The fortieth day after meeting Dr. Phinn found me seated with a West African President and the First Lady of the country outlining a vision that would allow me to be a blessing to the country and to advance the Kingdom of Heaven. This meeting was fruitful and later after becoming a fully fledged Ambassador, we would collaborate on many issues to help this African nation and many other nations in that region of the world.

It was a miracle! I, who had suffered beyond anything I could imagine during the previous five years, was in a foreign land talking about the problems and misfortunes of others as opposed to being totally self-absorbed. This I considered the miracle of miracles, a thing which took me beyond myself to fulfill a destiny that included uplifting God's people.

When the flight touched down at the airport on the fifty-sixth day after meeting Dr. Phinn and listening to him speak miracles into my life, I arrived at the United Nations Headquarters in New York to receive my United Nation's clearance badge and pin, capping off a whirlwind round of events. Miracle upon miracle had manifested itself into my life. I had been blessed tremendously and in turn, I became a blessing to many others.

On Sunday, January 23rd, the fifty-sixth day after meeting and hearing the spoken words and prayer of Dr. Phinn, I was appointed and sworn in as the Word of Life Ministries International/International Third World Leaders Association Ambassador to the United Nations Economic and Social Council (UNECOSOC). The appointment to Ambassador was granted by The UN Headquarters in New York.

Word of Life Christian Fellowship aka World of Life Ministries International is a Non-governmental Organization (NGO) in special consultative status with the Economic and Social Council of the United Nations and the first Full Gospel Ministry granted consultative status with the UN.

My church is a gospel filled church and you can feel the presence of God on any day; however, January 23, 2010 was a truly special day. You could feel the electricity bouncing from wall to wall, person to person, pulpit to congregation. Everybody present knew they were witnessing a miracle of God and every soul in this house of God was lifted. They had prayed with me and for me. Everybody knew my life's story. They'd seen my condition, they'd witnessed my shame, they had seen me down so low that up had been deleted from my vocabulary. They knew where I had been and they had seen me delivered. Together we rejoiced in the goodness of God, His power to heal and His ability to deliver us from all manner of evil. As one, we gave praise and thanksgiving for I had come full circle and the Lord had taken me from a place of abandonment, despair, depression, painful loneliness and shame and a broken heart and lifted me from the depths of despair to a place where I could shower His goodness around the globe.

I consider it an honor and a privilege to push forth the Global Health Agenda of the United Nations Economic and Social Council (UNECOSOC), taking on some of the biggest threats facing the world, such as Improving Health Outcomes of Women & Girls. My personal initiatives as Ambassador will include helping the UN further its Millennium Development Goals 2015 in the economic and social development of third world countries particularly in the areas of pharmaceuticals and emergency medical services.

My efforts will include fostering partnerships between the United Nations, private sector, foundations, community and government to maximize the outcomes for the world's most vulnerable people by identifying solutions to international economic, social and health problems.

In conjunction with women who have weathered the storm for many years, struggling with conditions that were sometimes more difficult than the ones I witnessed, we developed an agenda that is intended to be pleasing unto the eyes of the Lord.

I have learned many things on this journey none of which is more succinct than this fact: God answers every prayer and sometimes the answer is simply "NO"! Sometimes He shouts it, sometimes he whispers it, but in all cases you hear it loud and clear

It seemed that no matter how hard and long I prayed, God simply was not listening. I asked for the things I needed. My constant plea had been for my husband not to go to jail. When that failed, I prayed for God to let me keep my house. I had worked to help pay for that house as well. God kept right on moving and the long arm of the law took my house. I thought that Jackie and I would be together for a lifetime. He let the cancer come back in her body and she died. I watched as my son clung near death with Leukemia, and I prayed for a healing.

I was always praying for God to reach out and make something or somebody right. When I lost the ability to feel that depth of emotion, when nothing else mattered, it was at that moment when my eyes opened and my ears opened and I could see and hear for the first time that God had answered my prayer each and every time. Sometimes you just have to be still.

When I began to ask for peace of mind, understanding was delivered unto me. I understood that John was in jail but it was not a life sentence. Ten years were doable and Federal Prison was better than state prison. I may have lost the house but we were never homeless. Another house will come and we will not have to worry about it being taken from us. Jackie and I were together for a lifetime. Her lifetime. I may have wanted more but that was not left to me. God gives and God takes away. Jason may have had cancer but cancer did not have him. Times were rough and it was a struggle but he recovered and he is home with us every night. What I now know is that God answers in his own way and in his own time.

The measure of man is usually found in how well you respond to other life lessons. It is that we all need someone to hold our hand and sometimes we need a push up; we need someone to believe in us until we can believe in ourselves; that it is our duty to give until it hurts and then give more. It is our duty to recognize when we've been lifted and to understand that lifted does not necessarily mean the same to God as it means to us.

EMBASSY
PUBLISHING

Do you need a speaker?

Do you want Allison Wiley to speak to your group or event?
Then email Allison Wiley at: allison_wiley@yahoo.com
or use the contact form at: **www.beliftedtoday.org**

Whether you want to purchase bulk copies of *Lifted* or buy
another book for a friend, you can contact us at:
embassypublish@aol.com or call (817) 213-7767

**If you have a book that you would like to publish,
you may contact Embassy Publishing at (817) 213-7767
or email: embassypublish@aol.com**